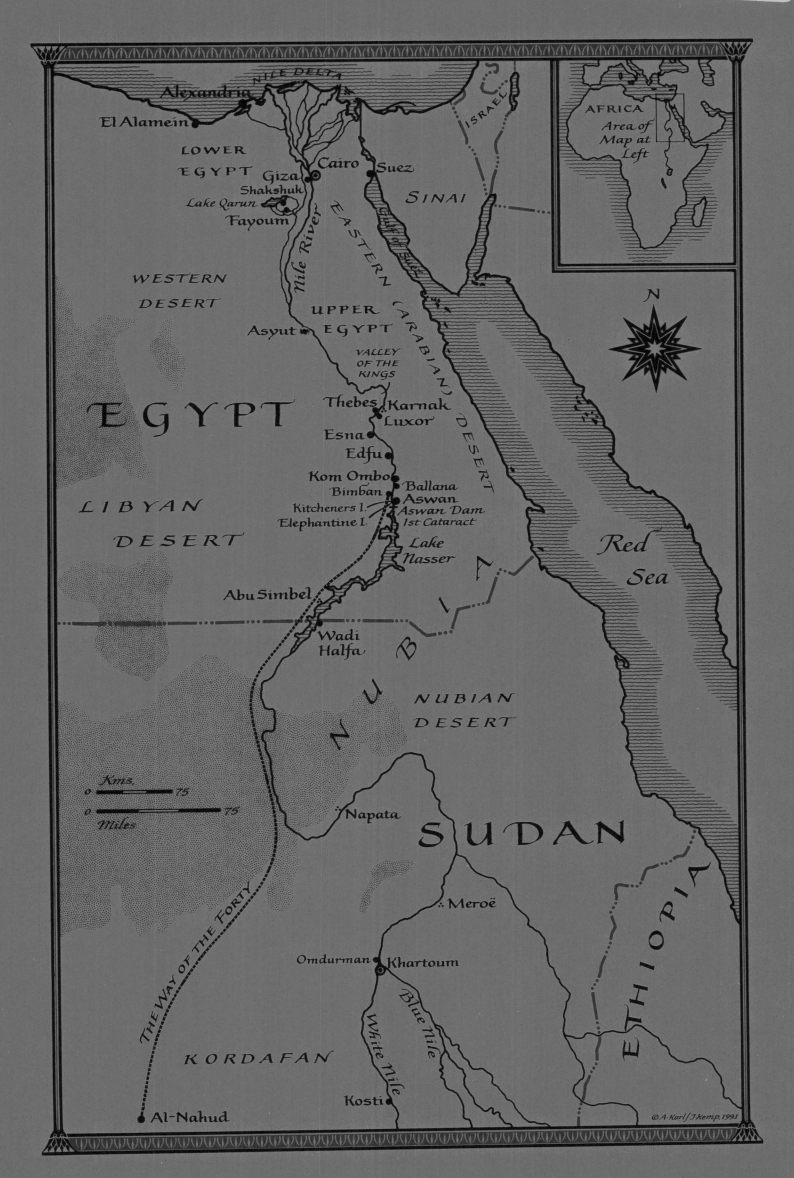

AFRICA
Area of
Map at
Left

N

EGYPT

LOWER
EGYPT

NILE DELTA

Alexandria
El Alamein

Cairo
Suez

Giza
Shakshuk
Lake Qarun
Fayoum

SINAI

ISRAEL

Gulf of Suez

WESTERN
DESERT

Nile River

UPPER
EGYPT

Asyut

VALLEY
OF THE
KINGS

Thebes   Karnak
Luxor
Esna
Edfu
Kom Ombo
Bimban   Ballana
Kitcheners I.   Aswan
Elephantine I.   Aswan Dam
                 1st Cataract
          Lake
          Nasser

EASTERN (ARABIAN) DESERT

LIBYAN
DESERT

Abu Simbel

Wadi
Halfa

N
U
B
I
A

Red
Sea

NUBIAN
DESERT

Kms.
0 ———— 75
0 ———— 75
Miles

Napata

SUDAN

Meroë

THE WAY OF THE FORTY

KORDAFAN

Omdurman Khartoum

White Nile
Blue Nile

ETHIOPIA

Kosti

Al-Nahud

© A·Karl/J·Kemp. 1991

EGYPT

To Peter Pawley

a very happy birthday to you!

With best wishes

Mary Cross

August 1991

Nantucket

Egypt

TEXT AND PHOTOGRAPHS BY MARY CROSS

HARCOURT BRACE JOVANOVICH · PUBLISHERS · NEW YORK · SAN DIEGO · LONDON

ALSO BY MARY CROSS

Behind the Great Wall: A Photographic Essay on China

Copyright © 1991 by Mary Cross

Requests for permission to make copies of any part of the work

should be mailed to:

Permissions Department, Harcourt Brace Jovanovich, Publishers, Orlando Florida 32887

Library of Congress Cataloging-in-Publication Data

Cross. Mary.

Egypt / Mary Cross. — 1st ed.

p.   cm.

Includes bibliographical references.

ISBN 0-15-145767-0

1. Egypt—Description and travel—1981 I. Title.

DT56.C7   1991

962.05′5—dc20   91-15074

CIP

First edition

A B C D E

HBJ

Maps by Anita Karl and James Kemp

Manufactured in Italy by Amilcare Pizzi, s.p.a., Milan

To Teddy

CONTENTS

AUTHOR'S NOTE

My deep affection for Egypt began in March, 1984. With my sister-in-law Margaret Bean, I embarked on a sixteen-day journey to Egypt. For Margaret, it was a returning pilgrimage. Seduced by memories of towering obelisks, swallow-winged feluccas, and graceful papyrus fronds, she had agreed to come once more. While I worked with my Hasselblad to capture vignettes of Egyptian life passing like scenes in a magic lantern show, she applied herself to the subtle colorations of brush and paint on paper.

At Giza we dutifully photographed each other on tourist camels, our heads crowned with white burnooses, playing at Lawrence of Arabia. Great pyramids loomed prominently in the background of our portraits of each other. In Cairo we went three times to the musty and cluttered, but astonishingly complete, Cairo museum which offers three millennia of pharaonic Egypt. Twenty miles out in the desert we savored the chaste simplicity of the ancient Old Kingdom monuments of Sakkara and Memphis.

After five days of frantic Cairo and side trips to its more serene environs, we flew to Luxor and Thebes, the ancient seat of government for pharaohs of the Middle Kingdom and the home of giant golden burial hills that guard the valleys of the Kings and of the Queens. Luxor is also the home of the magnificent temple palace of Karnak. For me, Karnak is like Chartres Cathedral—one of man's most mystical yet splendidly tactile creations—both great structures dedicated to manifestations of God. We arrived at eight in the morning before the hordes of tourists exploded into the enormous hypostyle hall of the great Temple of Amun. Quite alone in the huge colonnaded enclosure, we drank in the mysteries and holiness of this massive sanctuary, built by human ingenuity and punishing toil.

Steeped in the mythology of Egypt, I revelled in our guide's retelling of fanciful stories I had read as a child; of gods and their treacheries, their vengefulness, their stories of creation and their exotic loves and marriages.

On the eighth day of our journey we left behind the royal burial grounds in the violet-colored Theban hills and the haunting majesties of Karnak and Luxor temples. At sunset we embarked on a riverboat named *Isis*. The name rekindled memories of childhood myths. I had always been charmed by the powerful Egyptian legend of the Mother Goddess Isis who defeated the malevolent Set by miraculously reassembling the dismembered body of her husband, Osiris, making it possible for him to sire Horus, the falcon-headed god of the sky.

We were heading upstream towards Aswan, sailing among water hyacinths and feluccas, often passing other riverboats headed downstream towards Cairo. (Confusing and worth noting, one must constantly remember that "upper Egypt" is in the *south*.) On the deck we could see the unfolding panorama of timeless village life. For the sharecropping fellahin there is a fine line between survival and death, as thin as the gray thread that divides night from dawn.

The second day on the river, I received a radiogram from the ship's office. My mother was dead. She had died several days earlier, never waking out of a deep coma of three months duration. The funeral was scheduled for ten days hence at my childhood home in Kentucky. I would have to return from Egypt in order to get my children home from schools and colleges. My husband urged me to continue my trip until we reached Aswan. He assured me there was nothing I could do at home.

I remained on board ship. The waters of the life-giving Nile were part of a curative process; they bound up wounds, they provided me with a kind of serenity. In Egypt, it was hard to mourn my mother whose vitality and spirit had long ago left her body. Fantasizing, I would have loved her to resume her long storytelling afternoons from my childhood, one of the memories I most treasured. It was she who read endlessly to me of fairies and dragons and gods and goddesses. She imbued in me a love of narrative. Everything I saw on the Nile seemed part of the healing of my spirit.

On the river, the panorama of simple country life unfolded hypnotically. We moved slowly and there was time to savor the picture of women, unglazed waterjugs gracefully balanced on their heads, picking their way through reeds and cattails to the Nile's muddy edge. Scenes of donkeys and their fellahin masters bent over, hoeing beans, planting sugar cane, of mud houses and tall minarets—all passed by as I sat and watched and remembered. On the fifth day the river narrowed. We had arrived at Aswan. I left my sister-in-law and the benevolent protection of the *Isis* and flew back to Cairo to begin my funeral journey home.

As my plane took off, I looked down at the narrow, green ribbon of Nile fertility which so abruptly turns to brown. Suddenly I was seized with a powerful desire and determination to return and take a closer look at the people who dwell in the distant deserts of Egypt, hundreds of miles from the much beaten tourist tracks along the Nile.

The pictures in this book are the results of four journeys in 1984, 1988, 1989, and 1990.

Princeton, New Jersey   M.S.C.
March 1991

ACKNOWLEDGMENTS

My first thanks go to my dear friend, Katherine Hughes, who, eight years ago, first enticed me into the endlessly fascinating world of Near Eastern Studies. Special thanks, too, to my loving and caring sister-in-law, Margaret Bean, who first took me to Egypt in 1984.

There are several people without whose support and guidance this book would not have been written. They are: Professor Joseph Hobbs, distinguished expert on the Bedouin tribes of Egypt. He is a great scholar and a caring man to whom I am endlessly grateful; Professor Lanny Bell, former director of the Epigraphic Survey in Luxor, and presently Professor of Near Eastern Studies at the University of Chicago, for his friendship and his unstinting hospitality at Chicago House and for his help in reading my text. Affectionately greeted throughout Luxor and the West Bank as "Docktor Lanibell," few Westerners have established a closer bond with, and won such respect and affection from, the Egyptian people. I thank, too, his dear wife, Martha, who first introduced me to the works of early British travelers to Egypt, hidden away in the library of Chicago House. My thanks to Dr. John Swanson, director of Field Studies at the American University in Cairo, traveling companion and supportive friend, who generously shared his enormous energy, humor, and knowledge of the mysteries of St. Catherine's Monastery, guided me through the City of the Dead and the mosques of Islamic Cairo. I also thank archeologist Anthony Mills, genial host and director of the Dakhla project, who graciously offered me hospitality in his "dig house" in Bashendi, and provided me a bed from which I could see the moon.

I am deeply grateful to my friends and to the scholars at Princeton University who have so heroically given of their time and wisdom to advise me. They are: Professor Robert Fagles, distinguished poet and translator of the Greek classics and my dear friend and unfailing inspiration, who encouraged me at all stages of my effort. I thank him, too, for his poetic interpretation of the gates of the German cemetery at el-'Alamein; Professor John Waterbury, ever deeply supportive, who instructed me in the economics of developing countries and conceived the plan for an exhibition of my work at Princeton University; Professor Carl Brown, Director of the Program in Near Eastern Studies at Princeton University, who welcomed me into his classroom, gave me wise counsel and enthusiastically supported the public showing of my work; Professor Abraham Udovitch, Chairman of the Department of Near Eastern Studies at Princeton University, whose vivid course was my first introduction to Mediterranean Islam, and who has been gracious and supportive; Professor Margaret Larkin who generously shared information and insights on women and popular culture in contemporary Egypt. I thank, too, her husband, Muhammed Hussein, who was always a reliable backup for information on the *Hajj* and on village life.

I wish to express my thanks to Professor Charles Issawi and his wife, Janina, of Princeton University for their affectionate encouragement, and to Charles, particularly, for his eloquent lectures on the Economics of the Near East; to Professor Lila Abu-Lughod, my friend in Cairo and Princeton, who inspired and introduced me to the complex psychology of Bedouin and Egyptian women; to Professor

Lucette Valensi of the École des Hautes Études en Science Sociale in Paris, who made valuable suggestions about historic Cairo; to Princeton University doctoral candidate David Marmer, who, on short notice, contributed to my chapter on Islamic Cairo; to doctoral candidate, Mona Zaki, also of Princeton University, who checked facts and corrected errors in the Arabic language; and to Professor Julian Jaynes, who was always willing to take time from his search for wisdom among the signs and symbols of pharaonic Egypt to introduce me to new ideas. Finally, I am endlessly grateful to the superb collection at Princeton's Firestone Library and to the staffs of both the Department and the Program in Near Eastern Studies at the University.

I express my deep gratitude to the Egyptian government and its officials for granting me permission to enter the closed areas of Sinai, and for arranging military protection in remote parts of the desert. I am grateful for the kindness of the Honorable el Sayed Abdel Raouf El Reedy, Republic of Egypt Ambassador to the United States, who, together with Press Minister Mohamed Wahby, met me in Washington and helped pave the way to Sinai. I express appreciation, too, for the help of Egyptian Minister of Information, His Excellency Mr. Safwat El Sherif, and Major General Omar Soliman, Director, Military Intelligence, Arab Republic of Egypt, and to the five military escorts who accompanied me on the various segments of my trip in Sinai. I express greetings and thanks to His Excellency Munir Ahmad Muhammad Shash, Governor of North Sinai. I also express deep thanks to Dr. Wahbi Abdallah, Mr. Tarek Mansour, and Mr. Said Momtez, who briefed me on Bedouin life and customs, and to Mr. Mohamed Korayem, former Director of Economic Development in North Sinai and a staunch friend of the Bedouin. He was my mentor and tutor in North Sinai and he shared with me unique information on "outcast tribes" and customary law among the Bedouin. In the village of El Karoba, Sheikh Salam Arada invited us to sit around his fire and offered us the hospitality of his cardamon coffee. In South Sinai, I wish to express my deep appreciation to Monk-Priest Makarios, who spent endless hours showing us the Monastery and its priceless icons, and who gave us a private tour of the treasures in the superb library of manuscripts.

In the United States, my first thanks go to my beloved friend, former Under Secretary of State Richard Moose, whose enthusiasm and encouragement sustained me throughout. Richard introduced me to Egyptian Ambassador El Reedy and to the United States Ambassador to Egypt, Frank Wisner, as well as to United States Ambassador to the United Nations, Thomas Pickering and his wife, Alice. From his office in Cairo, Ambassador Wisner worried about my safety and safeguarded me in all my voyages in the desert. I am deeply grateful to the Ambassador and to his director of military security, Colonel Lemon. Thanks, too, to Marcelle Wahba, press attaché in the American Embassy in Cairo, who spent many hours working on my Sinai expedition. In New York City, the Pickerings took me under their warm and protective wings. As former Ambassadors to both Jordan and Israel, the Pickerings made many camping expeditions in Sinai. They got out their personal maps and historical data to instruct me in the places I needed to visit.

A number of scholars in Cairo and Luxor greatly illuminated my studies. They are Professor Timothy Mitchell of New York University, who led me to a better understanding of village people and agriculture along the Nile. Jean-Claude Vatin, Director of the Social Science Research Center in Cairo, introduced me to numerous scholars and experts on the sociology of Egypt. Elizabeth Wickett, expert on the folk culture of Egypt, instructed me in the culture of the *mulids*. My thanks, also, to Dr. Edward Brovarski, Research Curator, Department of Egyptian and Ancient Near Eastern Art, Boston Museum of Fine Arts, who led us through the tombs and temples of the Kings and Queens, and who provided brilliant and inspiring lectures on pharaonic Egypt. Thanks, too, to Egyptologist and psychotherapist, Dr. Del Nord, for her lyrical translations of hieroglyphics.

The American University in Cairo is an important presence in the Egyptian community. A number of people at the University helped my work. I am indebted to President Emeritus Richard F. Pedersen and his wife, Nelda, who introduced me to the Cairo community. I thank American University's distinguished expert on the Bedouin, Professor Donald Cole, for his vast knowledge of the desert people. Particularly, I am deeply indebted to the endlessly energetic and skillful Dr. Thomas Lamont, Director, New York office, American University in Cairo, who assumed enormous responsibility for implementing my plans. I cannot express the depth of my gratitude and appreciation for the remarkable connections and events that he brought about. Thanks to University trustee, John McCloy, who provided me with my first introduction to Tom Lamont and to the A.U.C.

A large number of public as well as private figures provided help in my writing, information, or in the exhibition of my work. They are George Beitzel, Sloan Bermann, Professor Robert Connor, Lynne Fagles, Annette Gonella, Paulina Gonzales, Lidia Harbat, Nicholas Katzenbach, Lois Keates, Mary Keeley, Bradford Kelleher, Afaf Mahfouz, Maggie Moose, Dr. James Peacock, Frederick Papert, and Jeffrey Zack.

The publication of this book has been preceded by exhibitions of my photographs. The Princeton University exhibition was conceived by Professor John Waterbury. In the selection of exhibition photographs, I was indebted to the indispensable artistic judgments of Carroll Bever, Judith Rulon-Miller, and Anne Reeves. The success of the Princeton exhibition was due in great measure to Ingrid Reed and Agnes Pearson. In the hanging, I was skillfully assisted by Guy Horner, Stephen and Jill Schreiber and Cay Mohrman. Thanks also to Don Havenick for his superb mounting and framing of exhibition prints. I also express my deep gratitude to Dr. Terry Waltz of the American Research Center in Egypt for his enthusiastic support of a New York City exhibition of my photographs.

I am indebted to that genius of book production, Harriet Ripinsky, without whose intricate planning and good judgment this book would never have gone to the printer. I am also thankful to Harriet's talented sister, Linda Ripinsky, who worked competently at all stages of the production effort. I will always value the warm and sensible counsel of Greer Allen, and my thanks go also to Sue Allen for her subtle insights into the spirit of my photographs. My gratitude goes to Anita Karl and James Kemp, who drew lovely maps to help the reader follow the progress of my story up the Nile River and through the deserts of Egypt. I am deeply grateful to my brilliant copy editor, Terese Kreuzer, who spotted errors and suggested alternative phrasing in the rough spots. I thank Lori Jacobs, who performed copy editing marvels in parts of the manuscript.

My special appreciation to David Pendlebury, the bibliographic genius at Philadelphia's Institute for Scientific Information, who searched his computer files at the University of Pennsylvania and provided me with a steady stream of papers and articles on the *fellahin* and the Bedouin tribes. Deep thanks to my literary agent, Connie Sayre, who unfailingly counselled and supported me in this effort. My friend, Stanley Karnow, with fortitude and humor, helped with early captions while his leg was encased in a cast. My text and captions were greatly strengthened by my dear friend and master of all knowledge, Alan Williams. Alan saved me from the "Herodotus trap." Thanks to Ann Vehslage, Ramsay Vehslage, and Ramsay Vehslage, Jr. who enthusiastically provided the benefit of their fine critical vision in helping choose the photographs for the book.

At my publisher, Harcourt Brace Jovanovich, I express my thanks to Corlies Smith, my understanding and supportive editor. He is a man of subtlety and wit and is unfailingly kind. Thanks, also, for the help of Alane Mason and for the artistic eye of Rubin Pfeffer.

I am eternally grateful to my friends and traveling companions who unfailingly corrected my memory and my lapses in remembering events. They are June Tower, who has always been a loyal friend, sensitive observer, and brave adventurer into Bedouin tented camps and villages. My thanks to her husband, Walter Tower, intrepid adventurer and tireless negotiator in the markets of the Middle East, who unfailingly sorted through the complexities of my Japanese camera equipment and shared Mounds bars and *mastabas*, to Jerry Cross, who provided *baksheesh* for my indigenous models at tombs and temples, to Joan Cross, who encouraged me to return, and to Marjorie Quine, seven times traveler to Egypt, expert scholar of Egypt's Old Kingdom, who shared her archeological knowledge, her cabin on the *Prince du Nil* and her reminiscences of our two common voyages. Thanks to her husband, Harvard University philosopher Willard Van Ormon Quine, who entertained me with songs from his childhood as we rattled across the Western Desert, and who brilliantly recited ''The Sultan's Turrets'' by lamplight in Bashendi. I thank Samir Abu Bakr el Said, my superbly competent and resourceful driver.

I acknowledge a very large debt of gratitude to Rochelle Lewis for her indefatigable efforts of typing and retyping my manuscript, and who rose from her deathbed to help me just prior to the manuscript deadline, to Adrienne Cannella, who so skillfully helped me to develop and organize my reference notes and bibliographic materials, and to Joann Scanlon who, over the past fifteen years, has brilliantly organized my photographic archives by means of her quick and ingenious retrieval system, to Elaine Kursch and Bruce Slater, who used their mastery of the computer to set type for the captions for my photographs, and to Emma Fried, who has helped me plan the organization and logistics of my Egyptian travels.

My mother died as I was beginning this project. My author's note does not even begin to express my debt to her for a lifetime of love and support and for her love of travel and adventure.

My greatest debt, as always, is to the members of my family. My daughters, Stuart, Ann, and Polly Warner encouraged me with their love and excitement over my photographs. My daughter, Ann, a woman of subtle judgment in both the world of vision and of the written word, helped refine my final choice of photographs and read through and made suggestions in my completed manuscript.

I am indebted to the patient advice of my husband, Theodore Cross, whose warm heart and wonderfully sunny spirit contributed so much to the development and organization of my thoughts. He was a constant and loving support in the execution of this project.

I am eternally grateful to all the friends and scholars who read, reviewed or advised me on various parts of my manuscript. But this work is mine, and if there are errors, they are my responsibility.

Cairo

◁◁ *Previous page:* The Mosque of Ahmad ibn Tulun was built in 876 A.D. Entering its vast, empty courtyard, one strongly feels the power and beauty of Islam. From the classical period of Islam, this is the oldest mosque in Egypt that still retains its original foundations and form. Its architectural style originated in Mesopotamia during the period of the Iraqi 'Abbasids who assumed leadership of the Islamic Empire in 750 A.D. The Mosque's builder, ibn Tulun, was one of the most important rulers in early Islamic history.

The present minaret was added in the thirteenth century and commands a dramatic view in every direction, and as far to the west as the great pyramids. The domed building in the central court is also a thirteenth-century addition. The Mosque encompasses an area of six-and-a-half acres.

Cairo

The Medieval City

By Middle Eastern standards, Cairo is a relatively new city. It was founded in 969 A.D., a full 350 years after Allah revealed Islam to the Prophet Muhammed. Despite its late start, Cairo quickly became a major commercial and cultural center of Islam. More than any other city in the medieval world, Cairo inspired great adulation. In the fourteenth century, the renowned Arab historian, ibn Khaldun, wrote this glowing account of the city he dearly loved:

> It is the metropolis of the universe, the garden of the world, the nest of the human species, the gateway to Islam, the throne of royalty: it is a city embellished with castles and palaces and adorned with monasteries of dervishes and with colleges lit by the moons and the stars of erudition.

Cairo was founded by the Fatimids, an unorthodox Muslim dynasty that swept eastward from Tunisia in the tenth century. Like Iranians of today, the Fatimids were inspired by their belief in the Shi'ite version of Islam. Rejecting Sunni beliefs that passed Muslim leadership to a series of caliphs, they claimed to be the sole legitimate Islamic rulers, due to their descent from the Prophet Muhammed through his daughter Fatima. Thereby, they challenged the established religious and political order of the Muslim world. During the century before their founding of Cairo, the Fatimids had secured control over much of the Mediterranean—Fatimid armies and navies had taken possession of Sicily, Sardinia, Corsica and Malta, had plundered the coasts of France and Italy, and had generally dominated the Barbary Coast from Morocco to Egypt.

The Fatimid city of Cairo has astrological roots. According to legend, the Fatimids, who were also dedicated students of the heavens, had arranged for some astrologers to pull on bell-ropes as a signal for the workmen to turn the first clods of earth for the building of the new city. Suddenly, a raven intervened by alighting on the rope and jingling the bells just as the planet Mars was rising on the horizon—hence the city's name of al-Qahirah, or Mars. Legend also suggests that the site for the city was the spot where the Arab soldiers who originally conquered Egypt in 640 A.D. found a dove sitting on a nest of eggs in the tent of their leader, 'Amr ibn al-'As. 'Amr at once declared the site sacred and Cairo became known as al-Fustat, or "The Town of the Tent."

The most sybaritic of monarchs ever to rule Cairo, the Fatimid caliphs inherited from their predecessors and rivals—the 'Abbasid caliphs of Baghdad—a society that was well advanced in luxurious living. The historian Ira Lapidus writes that, "emulating the rival 'Abbasid and Byzantine empires, the palace of the ruler was decorated with extraordinary splendor," replete with cascading fountains, golden ornaments, and precious gifts from foreign ambassadors.[1] The historian Philip Hitti notes that the 'Abbasids, who had once enjoyed scorpions, beetles and weasels as gourmet foods, in time came to feed their chickens on shelled nuts, almonds and milk. The well-to-do among the 'Abbasids dwelt in homes cooled by ice from the mountains, and fed on extracts of violets, bananas, roses and mulberries.

Alongside their appetite for luxury, the Fatimids were supporters of art and education. They built a number of great mosques and other architectural marvels. The most important Cairene monuments of the Fatimid caliphs included the soaring mosques of al-Azhar, al-Hakim, al-Aqmar, and al-Salih Tala'i, the magnificent northern city walls, the three city gates (Bab al-Futuh, Bab al-Nasr and Bab Zuwaylah), and the great mausoleums in the Qarafa, or Southern Cemetery. The Fatimids also founded the renowned al-Azhar University, which continues today to be one of the most venerable centers for religious studies in the Islamic world. Finally, as Shi'ite Muslims, the Fatimids encouraged the representation of human beings in art, boldly contravening Sunni (orthodox) interpretations of the teachings of the Prophet.

Toward the end of the tenth century, the empire of the Shi'ite Fatimids peaked under its fifth caliph, al-Aziz, an esteemed statesman, noted also for his gold-threaded turbans, the jewelled armor of his horses scented with ambergris, and the sumptuousness of his table. Al-Aziz's imperial interests extended beyond Egypt to Northern Africa and Southwest Asia. At one time, when he happened to look menacingly in the direction of Spain, the caliph in Cordoba wrote al-Aziz a sharp and threatening note. The potent and arrogant al-Aziz reportedly replied: "Thou ridiculest us because thou has heard of us. If we had heard of thee we would reply."

Al-Aziz's successor was the notorious al-Hakim (996–1021), one of the most bizarre characters in Egyptian history. Al-Hakim was famous for his destruction of the Holy Sepulchre in Jerusalem in 1009 A.D., an event which was a major cause of the Crusades. The leading historian of medieval Cairo, Stanley Lane-Poole, describes this most erratic and enigmatic man:[2]

> His strange face, with its terrible blue eyes, made people shrink; his big voice made them tremble. His tutor had called him "a lizard," and he had a creepy slippery way of gliding among his subjects that explained the nickname. He had a passion for darkness, would summon his council to meet at night, and would ride about the streets on his grey ass night after night, spying into the ways and opinions of the people under pretence of inspecting the market weights and measures . . . Officials of all grades were barbarously tortured and wantonly killed. A distinguished general, after putting down a rebellion which kept Egypt in a tumult for two years, happened to disturb Hakim when he was cutting up a murdered child, and paid for his indiscretion with his life.

But the mad caliph al-Hakim was an aberration. In general, the Fatimid Shi'ite caliphs were renowned for their religious and intellectual tolerance. They built a city of enormous power and wealth. From Cairo in the eleventh century, the Fatimids ruled an empire that extended almost three thousand miles from Tripoli to Damascus. Historian Hitti describes the splendid order and stability of this period. The streets of Cairo were often covered and lighted with lamps. Food and other goods were sold at fixed prices. Shopkeepers who cheated their customers were paraded on camels through the streets, made to ring bells and to confess their sins publicly. At night, the shops of the jewellers and moneychangers were left unlocked. As Bernard Lewis summarizes, "the Fatimid period was . . . an epoch of great commercial and industrial efflorescence."[3] One might have expected that the free-thinking traditions of Shi'ite culture under the Fatimid caliphs would have attracted great scholars to Cairo. But the rest of the Muslim world viewed the Fatimids and their messianic version of Islam with skepticism and apprehension, and thus Cairo developed a somewhat separate and isolated culture, not well integrated with the cosmopolitan cultures of Baghdad and Damascus. The triumphs of the Fatimids in architecture, textiles and pottery were impressive, but few of the great leaders of Arabic science, literature or scholarship emerged under their dynasty.

Despite their massive military powers, the Fatimid caliphs in Cairo, like the Mamluks who followed them, had no powers of religious revelation or interpretation. As custodians of the faith, the job of the caliphs was to make war against nonbelievers and suppress heresies within the ranks at home. Their dynasty lasted for two hundred years. But under al-Hakim's son, al-Zahir, a weak carbon copy of the strong but demented father, corruption ruled the court. The slaves of the palace mutinied, and Syria was in revolt.

According to the historian, Lane-Poole, al-Zahir amused himself with dancers and young girls, whom he bricked up to starve to death in his mosque. During al-Zahir's rule, Berbers overran the Nile Delta and destroyed the irrigation system in order to starve the peasants. Upper Egypt was lost to the Sudanese, and Turks looted the capital at Cairo. This was also a period of great famine in Egypt. Contemporary reports say that people in the city actually kidnapped and ate each other and that human flesh was sold by butchers. This terrible famine did not come to an end until the bountiful harvest of 1073 A.D. The Fatimid dynasty finally fell in 1171 A.D., when the great Saladin ("rectitude of the faith"), a Kurdish general in the army of the caliph of Baghdad, led the invasion of Egypt. With only nominal allegiance to Baghdad, Saladin established the new Ayyubid dynasty. According to historians, his coming to power was so peaceful that "not even two goats locked horns." The change in dynasties was symbolized by the simple act of removing the name of the Fatimid caliph from the Friday prayer. Saladin replaced Shi'ite beliefs at court with Sunni orthodoxy, and once more raised Cairo to the rank of an imperial capital. Saladin was said to be the master of espionage. He excelled in the manufacture and use of poisoned knives, and developed an elaborate carrier pigeon system that provided him strategic information which appeared to emanate from super-natural sources. Using these remarkable powers, Saladin invaded Syria, waged successful campaigns against Richard the Lion-Hearted in the Third Crusade, and declared himself a sovereign and independent ruler. Saladin was a noble figure with an impeccable code of honor in dealing with his foes. When he learned, during the Battle of Jaffa, that Richard's horse had been killed under him, the Sultan sent a groom leading two fresh Arabian mounts.[4] Saladin was not merely a great warrior and leader of Sunni Islam, but he also devoted himself to public works. He constructed great dikes, canals and mosques. His greatest architectural achievement was the Citadel of Cairo, which he built with stones removed from some of the smaller pyramids at Giza. He was also a patron of scholars and theologians. Saladin's dynasty came to an end in 1250 A.D., with the coming to power in Cairo of the Turkish slaves, or Mamluks.

Both the Fatimid dynasty and the Ayyubid dynasty which followed, used Turkish and Circassian slaves as the backbone of their armies. These slaves, known as Mamluks ("one who is owned"), revolted, removed the last of the Ayyubids, and established themselves as a military aristocracy that ruled Cairo and Egypt for over 250 years until the Ottoman Turkish conquest at the beginning of the sixteenth century. During this period (1260–1517), the Mamluks produced a succession of outstanding warriors. Through their military prowess, the Mamluks rid Egypt and the Levant of the Crusader armies that had threatened the region for two centuries and, more importantly, spared Cairo from the devastation that befell Baghdad by repelling four Mongol invasions. In the most glorious of their campaigns, the Mamluks marched on Syria and routed the Mongols at Goliath's Well in 1260 A.D. Later, their soldiers swam the Euphrates and once more defeated the Mongols at Bire in 1273. Because of these momentous victories and the resulting political stability of Egypt, Cairo experienced a golden age of economic and cultural development and emerged as the center of the Islamic world.

The most famous of the sultans to rule Mamluk Cairo was al-Nasir, who governed from 1303–1340. A short man, lame in one foot, al-Nasir had a great taste for architectural beauty and extravagant living. In his desert expeditions, his table was supplied with fresh vegetables from a traveling garden carried on forty camels. At his son's wedding, 20,000 animals were slain and devoured in the Royal Palace, which was lit by a thousand candles. When al-Nasir made his pilgrimage to Mecca, a retinue of 600 camels bearing food, vegetables, and flowers followed him across the desert. Yet al-Nasir was even more famous for his important public works. He dug an unprecedented canal connecting Alexandria with the Nile, a work of one hundred thousand men. He built thirty mosques in Cairo and constructed an aqueduct from the Nile to the capital. He developed the Southwestern Delta of the Nile, planted tens of thousands of fruit trees in the former desert, and created a hundred new villages for the Egyptian peasants.

The twelve successors of al-Nasir were less distinguished. Nevertheless, they successfully performed the primary responsibilities of maintaining law and order, collecting taxes, keeping the peasants working, and providing recruits for military campaigns. Indeed, this long period of Mamluk rule produced cultural and architectural achievements unparalleled in the medieval world. Not since the days of Hellenistic Alexandria had literature and the arts flourished in Egypt as they did in Mamluk Cairo. Among the most important architectural splendors of this period are the Mosque and Mausoleum of Barquq which took twelve years to build and was completed in 1411, the Mosque *Khanqah* and Tomb of Sultan Barsbay (1432) and the *Madrasa* and Tomb of Sultan Qaytbay (1472–74), all found in Cairo's Eastern Cemetery.

By the fourteenth century, the orderly grid of streets characteristic of Fatimid Cairo had been largely replaced by a labyrinth of narrow, covered streets, alleys, markets and courtyards. Nonetheless, in the words of the historian-philosopher ibn Khaldun, Cairo remained "the glory of Islam and the orchard of the world." The city was richly endowed by the Mamluks with libraries, teachers, scholars, booksellers, orphanages and hospitals. Through its warehouses, bazaars, inns and caravanseries, Cairo's merchants, bankers, moneychangers and customs inspectors conducted commerce with the great and far-away ports of India and China.

Physically, the Mamluks had re-created a magnificent city of high, yellow walls embellished with turrets, roofed-over balconies, open courtyards, secret doors, latticed windows, and incense-scented bazaars piled high with copper pots and silk brocades. On the streets of Cairo, the traveler from Italy or Spain was likely to see brides carried on litters and dressed in silks from Armenia. He would also view sellers of musk, myrrh and melons, and long processions of drums and pipes followed by laughing hordes of little boys, still dressed as girls to ward off the Evil Eye.

However, this period also witnessed the cruelty of the Mamluk military élite. They were known to cut people up with their knives or pull them apart with their horses. Proudly wearing their long swords, thick trousers and veils of mail, they rode through the teeming streets of Cairo, more or less indifferent to the people along the way. If they crushed a lame beggar on their way to the polo fields of the Sultan, so be it.

Seven years after Sultan al-Nasir's death in 1341, the dreaded Black Death reached Cairo. According to contemporary accounts, one to two thousand people died daily, the streets were piled high with unburied corpses, and Cairo was temporarily reduced to a ghost city, having lost almost half its population of five hundred thousand people. Tragically, the Bubonic plague returned twice more within the next decade. Amidst the stench of fetid streets and the ever-present odor of camel skins and stoves fired with cow dung, the Mamluk military élite continued to maintain civilian power through bribery and fear.

Despite the decline in population from its one-half million peak prior to the plague, the city was temporarily revitalized in the fifteenth century. Even after such adversity, Cairo remained an urban achievement more significant than that of either London or Paris, which did not reach populations of two hundred thousand until the sixteenth century. One historian wrote in 1481 "if it were possible to place all the cities of Rome, Milan, Padua and Florence together, they would not contain the wealth and population of the half of Misr (Cairo)."[5]

In 1498, a revolutionary event changed the course of the history of Cairo. Vasco da Gama, the Portuguese navigator, sailed around the Cape of Good Hope and landed in India, thus establishing a new trade route to the East. Most of the pearls, spices and silks from the Orient that had once traveled through Cairo were eventually carried on the new route. The Mamluks, who had always claimed the largest share of the profits from trade in return for military protection, compensated for this grave loss in their revenues by further tightening the screws on the Egyptian peasants. A French consul reported in the early sixteenth century:

The greed of the Mamluks is never satisfied until the fellahin are sucked dry . . . In Cairo, they slaughter men like beasts. Officers, who make their rounds day and night, hold their courts in the street, condemn the accused, and have them hanged at once. A man supposed to have money is denounced by some enemy and summoned to the bey; if he refuses to go, or denies his wealth, he is thrown onto the ground and given a bastinado of two hundred strokes, if he is not executed at once.

In 1517, the same year that Martin Luther posted his paper proclaiming the Reformation, Cairo was conquered by the Ottoman Turks. This marked the end of Mamluk rule and the suspension of Egyptian independence. From the sixteenth through the eighteenth centuries, Cairo, which had stood for two hundred and fifty years as the most glorious Islamic city of medieval times, became a mere provincial capital of the Ottoman Empire. Like Damascus, Medina, and Baghdad, Cairo was controlled by viceroys backed by armies of occupation dispatched from the Ottoman capital of Constantinople. The power held in Constantinople and the impotence of Cairo during these three centuries is reflected in a letter addressed by the Ottoman Sultan Suleiman the Magnificent, (1520–1566) to Francis I, King of France:

> I who am the Sultan of Sultans, the sovereign of sovereigns, the dispenser of crowns to the monarchs on the face of the earth, the shadow of God on earth, the Sultan and sovereign lord of the White Sea and of the Black Sea, of Rumelia and of Anatolia, of Karamania, of the land of Rum, of Zulkadria, of Diarbekir, of Kurdistan, of Azerbijan, of Persia, of Damascus, of Aleppo, of Cairo, of Mecca, of Medina, of Jerusalem, of all Arabia, of Yemen, and of many other lands which my noble forefathers and my glorious ancestors (may God light up their tombs!) conquered by the force of their arms and which my August Majesty has made subject to my flaming sword and my victorious blade, I, Sultan Suleiman Khan, son of Sultan Selim Khan, son of Sultan Bayezid Khan: To thee, who art Francis, King of the land of France.[6]

Under the Ottoman pashas in Cairo, the great figures of the Fatimid and Mamluk periods were entirely missing. Scholars have long maintained that this was, therefore, a period of cultural decline. Literature and the arts were no longer stimulated by the luxurious courts of the pashas; many of the great mosques fell into disrepair or were demolished to facilitate the construction of new streets; irrigation canals deteriorated, much land went out of cultivation, and public works were generally neglected. Moreover, the discovery of the Cape route to India had undermined the caravan trade that had previously been the economic strength of Cairo. However, current scholars are beginning to revise the perception of cultural decline during the Ottoman period. For example, André Raymond has pointed out that new architectural styles were imported for vast Ottoman-style mosques, and that public works such as fountains (*sabils*) and hospitals were continually endowed.[7] Nevertheless, while Cairo did continue to produce arts and learning, it was clearly not the rich cultural center of previous centuries.

Toward the end of the eighteenth century, the decay of the Ottoman Empire was apparent. The eyes of England turned to Egypt. A British merchant declared "we shall unite the Ganges, the Nile and the Thames and drink England's health on the top of the Pyramids." But Napoleon Bonaparte had similar plans. He dreamed of menacing the British in India by establishing a trade route through Egypt that would compete with the new British route around the Cape of Good Hope. The French general concluded that he could easily defeat the increasingly decadent descendants of the old Mamluk military élite, which still defended Egypt. Armed with 36,000 men and memories of the conquests of Alexander and Caesar, Napoleon arrived in Egypt in 1798. At the Battle of the Pyramids, at least six thousand cavalry engaged in combat on each side. In what historians call the last great cavalry charge of the Middle Ages, the Mamluks were massacred. Wearing their splendid turbans and gorgeous robes, flying colorful silken pennants over the heads of their horses, and carrying sabers in their hands, four thousand Mamluks went down in dust and smoke before the cannons of the French. The battle had been decided in a little less than an hour, and barely two hundred French had been killed. Moreover, the Mamluk cavalry had brought into battle their saddlebags full of gold coins. The French grenadiers became rich men as they fished in the Nile for the gold-laden bodies of drowned Mamluks. Napoleon marched into Cairo. It had already been taken over by looting mobs.

The French were not long to remain masters of Egypt. Ten days after Napoleon's victory in the Battle of the Pyramids, Lord Nelson virtually destroyed the French fleet at the Battle of the Nile. Now cut off from France, Napoleon realized that he would not be able to hold Cairo against the combined allied forces of the Turks and the British. So he hurried back to France, leaving his marshals and troops behind. In March, 1801, the French expeditionary force was defeated by the British and the Turks at the Battle of Alexandria. A hungry and battered Cairo was besieged and returned once more to Turkish control. According to contemporary accounts, the French, who were immensely unpopular in Cairo, "sailed from the shores of Egypt leaving behind the native women they had married to be sewn up in sacks and drowned by their angry relatives."

The modern history of Cairo begins with Albanian-born Muhammed 'Ali, an officer in the Turkish army that had helped drive Napoleon out of Egypt. Born in 1769, the same year as Napoleon, Muhammed 'Ali gradually established the independence of Egypt. He first crushed the Mamluks, who had continued to be feudal owners of much Egyptian land. As a lesson to those Mamluks who might defy him, he tortured and murdered his captives and then publicly displayed their heads stuffed with straw. Muhammed 'Ali was then promptly elected Pasha. When the British attacked Egypt in 1807, Muhammed 'Ali defeated their armies, sold many of them into slavery, and lined the streets of his victory parade with four hundred and fifty British heads on poles. Not surprisingly, British accounts of nineteenth-century Cairo appear motivated more by their contempt for the Egyptians than a concern for accurate reporting. One British visitor to the Egyptian court in the late nineteenth century described a Cairo procession of whirling dervishes:

> About noon, the Khedive arrived, and alighted at his tent. Soon afterwards a confused murmur arose, announcing that the procession of dervishes was coming . . . They plunged along, their bodies swaying, their eyes rolling, and mouths foaming . . . Many were crushing live serpents in their hands or tearing them to pieces with their teeth and devouring them ravenously; some were eating glass and fire; some were thrusting spikes of steel clean through their cheeks and arms; some were wildly beating tom-toms or shaking rattles; some were gashing their faces and breasts with knives and scimitars.[8]

Although he was illiterate, Muhammed 'Ali was a man of genius and courage. He occupied the Sudan, divided the Bedouin, warred successfully against the Wahhabis of Arabia and secured control of both coasts of the Red Sea. Now considered the father of modern Egypt, 'Ali modernized the army, built factories and shipyards, greatly expanded the production of cotton, and promoted learning by founding schools of medicine, importing foreign technicians, and sending Egyptians to study in France. Finally learning to read at age forty, this remarkable man abolished the unjust flogging of the peasants, and won respect for the Egyptian people. Under Muhammed 'Ali, the ancient Arabic proverb still governed life in Cairo: "Man's fate depends on his place in society." Yet, through a period of four thousand years of Egyptian history, Muhammed 'Ali was the first ruler to guarantee the civil rights of all classes of peoples and religions. Eventually, 'Ali became Viceroy of Egypt and wrested undisputed control of Egypt from the Turks. The dynasty he established—the Khedives—lasted until the overthrow of King Farouk in 1952.

The Modern City

The history of Islamic Cairo was an epic story of the extravagant deeds of the Fatimids, the Ayyubids, the Mamluks, and the extraordinary Egyptian emancipator, Muhammed 'Ali Pasha. The city's history was also a story about the splendors of medieval architecture and the glories of Arab science, culture and theological learning which took place during the half dozen centuries that followed the death of the Prophet. Thanks to the armies of the Mamluks who saved Cairo's historic monuments from the Mongols, the Citadel of

Saladin, the Mosque of ibn Tulun, and the *Madrasa* of Sultan Hasan stand, today, as monuments to the creativity and ambitions of the great sultans and caliphs of medieval Egypt. Amidst its diverse architectural styles of neo-Islamic, neo-Venetian and Ottoman baroque, Cairo continues to be the premier cultural and intellectual center of the Middle East.

Yet, this mega-city of the Muslim world (twice the size of its nearest contenders, Istanbul and Tehran) is no longer seen as ibn Khaldun's garden of the world. Cairo today undergoes the tribulations of all third-world cities. Its population doubling over the last twenty-five years has created an atmosphere of congestion that overshadows its past splendor. It is plagued by air pollution, noise, poverty, overcrowding and absence of green space. It is said that in Cairo half the people live on the rooftops and the other half in the city dumps or in the tombs on the outskirts of the city.

Some years ago, Professor John Waterbury observed that Egypt was locked inextricably in the grip of three great crises: transportation, housing and hostilities with Israel. The quarrels with Israel come and go, but the other two crises are ubiquitous and intractable. Perhaps the most visible of these is transportation. Writing in 1972, Professor Waterbury describes the bus in Cairo:

> Take, for instance, the bus—luckily for you figuratively and not literally. It is rumored that Cairo buses, when new, are taken at night into a huge empty lot and driven into each other until their windows are popped out, their lights smashed, and their chassis have taken on the proper shape, suggestive of a red sack of melons on wheels. New horns are installed with a husky, slightly prehistoric wheeze, the rear and front doors are wrenched away, and the whole super-structure is tilted about 45 degrees to starboard. With this preparation the fleet is ready to take to the road and face the hordes.[9]

In recent years, the macabre world of Cairo bus transportation has been enhanced and complicated by an explosion in the number of taxis. A taxi ride can be both painful and terrifying. It is often easier to walk than to take a taxi or a bus. Traffic in Cairo moves very fast with little regard for stop signs or red lights. A pedestrian crossing an intersection is truly taking his life in his feet.

Congestion in Cairo comes in all varieties and gives the city a special quality. Visitors immediately notice that streets in the city are not simply used by millions of cars, busses, mini-busses, donkey carts and Japanese three-wheelers. They are also employed as pedestrian ways, short-term parking lots, and as real estate supporting stationary juice shops and fruit carts. Cairo's street vendors add their poetry to the scene. At the end of the winter season, the orange vendor sadly calls out "Farewell, O oranges." The melodious call of the tomato-seller is "Jewels, O fine tomato." Anything made in the west—sunglasses, ties or watches—are hawked under the melodious and irresistible call of "Ya nylon."[10]

On my first visit to Cairo in the early 1980's, I saw five members of an Egyptian family happily taking tea as they squatted in the median between two horrendous lines of traffic on a major Cairo boulevard. Some years later at the Ramses Hilton, I looked down on rooftops where peasants, chickens, and goats all shared the same living space. Only a short block behind that five-star hotel lies a squalid, slum neighborhood, the Bulaq district, where families live five and six to a room. It is common to see flocks of sheep marked for the slaughterhouse being driven through Cairo's central shopping and business area past airline offices and expensive stores selling Rolex watches. On equal terms, the sheep and goats compete for space on Cairo's streets with thousands of sleek Mercedes-Benzes and the donkey-pulled carts of street vendors selling kebabs, *kaffiyahs* and plastic sunglasses.

A signal triumph in the battle against congestion is the new Cairo subway system. It is clean, quiet and civilized. Construction of the subway was intended to greatly reduce surface traffic. Instead, congestion has become worse. Also, the subway has exacerbated conflicts over women's rights. In order to protect women against sexual harassment, the first car of every train is reserved for females. One modernist objects: "This is a harem on wheels." A commentator in the *Egyptian Gazette* writes: "This pulls us back into the dark ages of segregation and even humiliates our women, treating them as weak and subordinate." To top it off, the Islamic fundamentalists object to women riding the subway at all: "Women are invading the public space and should be home with their children."[11]

But the main source of congestion in Cairo is not its vehicles, but its people. One of the most densely populated cities in the world, its older quarters often house up to 32,000 people per square mile. In the poorer neighborhoods the garbage is piled high because there is no place to put it, and the streets are swarming with children. Possibly a million people in Cairo—particularly the immigrants from the villages who amount to 10 percent of Cairo's annual population increase—live in shacks, shanty towns and other forms of illegal housing.

Fortunately, Egyptians are extremely sociable and tolerant people. Since Cairo is so severely overcrowded, its citizens have no choice but to accept close personal interaction with others. Cairenes are the most patient people on earth. They have an astonishing ability to put up with almost unendurable delays in the delivery of government services and permits. For the average Egyptian, just waiting in line to buy sugar or bread from a government store may take several hours. There is an almost daily breakdown in the delivery of rudimentary services. The electricity stops working, water supplies fail, plumbing falls apart, repairs on housing are never made, and the government store is likely to run out of necessities, such as kerosene or flour. Permits for a cabby license require six forms and twenty signatures at five different government offices. At the end of weeks of temper-trying paperwork, a discouraged Cairene may discover that one bureaucrat wrote his name in the wrong place or filled out a form incorrectly. Stoically shrugging off his hardships, the petitioner begins anew, and usually with a smile. Only patience and humor enable him to survive the daily adversities assaulting him from every side. There is a sweet, Chaplinesque quality that says "What is bad may get worse, but I will deal with it. Life will go on."

Especially among the middle and upper classes, mothers and fathers in Cairo live and dream for the future of their children. The universal hope and prayer is that their youngsters will do well in secondary school examinations, be admitted to one of the better universities, and embark on a professional career. To this end, huge sacrifices are made. After long hours of labor, the mother returns home, cares for and feeds perhaps six or seven children and supervises their homework. The father will often work one job in the morning and drive a cab for four or five hours in the afternoon to earn the money needed for the education of the children.

Population experts predict that Cairo can't be saved. Each time Cairo builds a new bridge or underpass to relieve the terrible traffic, more traffic is inexorably attracted, so that with each new improvement, congestion is made progressively worse. Surely the city must collapse by the sheer weight of the numbers of its people, vehicles and the baneful effects of rising sewage water and eroding salts. But it never does. Even in the eleventh century, under the Fatimids, Cairo apparently had a population of one million people. At that time it was probably the largest city in the world. Therefore, although Cairo today is a bursting mega-city of almost intolerable congestion and insoluble problems, it will survive as it has for the past ten centuries.

Moreover, Cairo remains an utterly beautiful and exciting city. It is a city of opera houses, famous hotels, incomparable museums, giant department stores, tree-lined avenues and sumptuous restaurants. Surrounding its magnificent arches, gates, minarets, cupolas and galleries are side streets and bazaars alive with commerce and packed high with bags of cinnamon, ginger and saffron as they were eight centuries ago. As always, the Khan al-Khalili, a bazaar which began as a caravansary in the fourteenth century, is bulging with Turkish hassocks, hand-crafted, burnished copper and bracelets of glittering gold.

In many ways, life in Cairo today is best told in terms of the history of the woman in Muslim society. Under the pharaohs, women in Egypt were treated as helpmates but never as chattels. They held positions of some importance both in religion and politics. And, like their husbands, they sat on thrones, though in Egyptian sculpture, the queen figures were usually represented somewhat smaller than the kings.

Hatshepsut ruled as a queen, wearing a beard to prove her equality with men. Yet, in the Egyptian world of the seventh century before the rise of Islam, women were wholly degraded and had no rights that a man needed to respect. It was Islamic law under the teachings of Muhammed that conferred some rights on women, including a fixed right of inheritance, prohibition of forced marriages, the right to earn an independent living, and, most importantly, the recognition of women as human beings instead of as chattels. Yet, according to the teachings of the Prophet, women were distinctly inferior to men and subject to physical discipline if they failed to be obedient or submissive. The *Qur'an* provided:

> The men are placed in charge of the women, since God has endowed them with the necessary qual-
> ities and made them breadearners. The righteous women will accept this arrangement obediently, and
> will honor their husbands in their absence, in accordance with God's commands. As for the women
> who show rebellion, you shall first enlighten them, then desert them in bed, and you may beat them as a
> last resort.[12]

Although the Islamic rules imposing inferior status on women—male guardianship, polygamy, seclusion and the unilateral right of repudiation of marriage—are observed in Egypt, that country has been the central force in the emancipation of women in the Arab world. In Egypt, equality of women's rights in matters of education, child care, family planning, and employment have been guaranteed by law. The constitution of Egypt has sweeping provisions calling for equality between the sexes except in matters that relate to the *shari'a*, or religious canons governing the status of women in the home, family and marriage. One of the landmarks of modern Cairo is a monumental statue, the *Revival of Egypt*. This sculpture, representing a revitalized Egypt, is of a peasant woman resolutely gazing into the future beneath the folds of an uplifted veil. Even some Muslim conservatives declare that the glories of medieval Cairo—reflected in the age of the Prophet—will not occur without major change in the education and prospects of Egyptian women.[13]

The literature on women in Cairo is elusive and full of contradictions. The best way to present the lower, middle-class *baladi* woman is to describe the public ideals by which she lives. The realities are often very different. In theory, she will be modest and diffident. She will lower her gaze in public and never display her arms, legs or bosom. Neither she nor her husband will show love or affection in the presence of strangers. As a woman, she will be judged, and judge herself, by whether she bears children, especially sons. She may not divorce her husband except for non-support, dangerous behavior, contagious disease or desertion. Particularly if she is a young, unmarried woman, her relatives, male and female, will monitor her movements to make sure there are no illicit relations or appearances of impropriety. As a married or unmarried woman, she will always be admired if she expresses a robust anger, if not violent reaction, to any flirtation from a male. If she deviates even slightly from the prescribed code of modesty, this will be taken as an invitation to sexual intimacy. She may be subjected to wife beating, or "disciplining", which will be considered a positive expression of love and affectionate jealousy. As a married woman, she will have regular visits from her husband's male relatives. She will always show them effusive hospitality, and she will enthusiastically discourage them from leaving her husband's house. Elderly parents will almost always live with her and she will seek their counsel and respect. But there may be undercurrents of friction. There is an old Egyptian proverb, "Your mother-in-law is a fever, your husband's sister is a poisonous scorpion and your father-in-law is a snake behind the water jar."

When a woman is married, she will submit to the *dukhla*, a ceremony in which the wedding guests if not the community at large, acknowledge her virginity. If she is not a virgin, it is likely that a midwife or other person will be hired to falsely testify to her virginity. Today, the rite of the *dukhla* is disappearing among middle and upper class women. After marriage, the wife will probably live with her mother-in-law until the birth of the first child. Commonly and preferably, her husband will be a close relative. (About 30 percent of Cairene marriages are within the kin group.) Probably she won't be divorced (the divorce rate is only 3 percent), but if she should be divorced or if, in the rare case, she becomes a co-wife in a polygamous marriage, she will be entitled to support from her husband. If she is widowed, Egyptian law entitles her to support from her husband's male relatives, but this stipend will be inadequate and won by her only after a lengthy legal battle. As a married woman, her children will accompany her almost everywhere.

Even among the lower classes, marriage must be observed with pomp and ceremony. The poor save for years in order to finance the wedding of a child. In a city where most people are poor, the marriage ceremony may cost several thousand dollars. As a result, couples from the poorer quarters of Cairo continue working after marriage. But if a man can afford to maintain a household in which his women do not work, they won't. So, paradoxically, wealthy women are most limited in their ability to leave the household and take employment. There is, however, a group of westernized women exposed to higher education who have professions and aspirations that take them outside the house. But for the vast majority of women, the most important thing in life will be family.[14]

In recent years, large numbers of Cairo women have opted for a new form of modest, Muslim dress consisting of head covers and long-sleeved, ankle-length gowns. In the city, this practice, known as veiling, is observed by women of all classes, including a large number of university professors and members of parliament. Less restrictive than traditional dress in more conservative parts of the Muslim world (where veils completely cover all but the eyes), Islamic dress in Egypt is, nevertheless, a focus of much controversy, for there are many Egyptians who view the practice of veiling as a despised symbol of the oppression of women in Arab societies. However, the vast majority of Egyptians—including most Egyptian women— would dispute this charge. For many women who veil, the head covering not only establishes their Muslim identity; it is also a statement of personal autonomy, respectability and independence. Paradoxically, the veil gives women greater protection against male harassment and thereby allows them to move about more freely in public. Women who wear western dress are much more vulnerable to harassment in the streets or subways. Generally speaking, conservative women in Cairo advocate veiling as an expression of religious piety, a return to national identity and an expression of anti-western sentiment. Not only do they wear the head scarf, long sleeves and long skirt, but they may also wear a face veil and gloves. This is in sharp contrast to the beautifully embroidered new style of headdress which has come to be known as "Islamic chic."[15] In both the most élite and the poorest quarters of Cairo, women are not much affected by Islamic chic. In the former, they continue to wear fashionable, expensive European clothes, and in the latter, as ever, they cover their heads and dress with a long piece of black cloth called the *milayah*.

The *Qur'an* confers responsibility on men to support their wives and families. Egyptian women value men who make money and are competent and generous providers for their families. The traditional man in Cairo firmly believes in his natural rights and authority over his wife. (The *Qur'an* provides: "Men have a rank above them," Surah 2:228). He will be keenly interested in his wife's personal attractiveness yet he may well be rude to her, as well as to other women, if they wear extravagant, western dress or revealing clothing. If his wife wishes to work, he will probably oppose it since he will be convinced that this employment will cause her to lose her femininity, limit her duties to the children, and curtail her ability to fulfill his entitlement to peace, attention and contentment at home. In the husband's view, her outside employment may expose her to the attentions of other men and also reflect adversely on his honor as a provider. Yet, if her work is financially necessary, he will grudgingly agree to it since times are hard and her job will help provide for the children's education and thereby strengthen the family.[16] In Egypt, as in most Muslim societies, the good of society as a whole takes a back seat to honor and family.

Egyptian men rarely visit with their friends at home. Instead, Cairo contains thousands of *qahwahs* or coffee houses. These coffee shops form an important gathering spot for the male Egyptian. In cities and in small towns, men go to the *qahwahs* to smoke, to gossip, to discuss women and to play cards and backgammon. Each man brings with him his own pipe and tobacco. The shopkeeper also keeps several waterpipes for smoking both Persian tobacco and hashish. Men from the poorer quarters and tradespeople frequent coffee shops in the afternoon and evening. A certain coffee house in Cairo will become known as a meeting spot for emigrés from a particular village or region in Upper Egypt. New arrivals in Cairo often locate relatives and friends from back home by visiting a designated *qahwah*.

Coffee was imported into Egypt at the beginning of the sixteenth century. Its use became the subject of frequent and acrimonious disputes among the learned and the devout. Many doctors and scholars felt coffee was an intoxicant and should, therefore, be unlawful for Muslim use. During the next hundred years, coffee was banned and then legalized once again. Many of the faithful argued that, because coffee repelled sleep, it helped the devout to stay awake for their nightly devotions. The coffee in Egyptian *qahwahs* is generally very strong and served with sugar.

It is my observation that in most settings, the men of Cairo are a very relaxed and good-natured group. Affability and expressions of fraternity seem to be almost universal. Men in Cairo are humorous, gregarious and they laugh a lot. In Baghdad, it is said, men in the parliament bow, click their heels and never make jokes or speak without asking permission. In the Egyptian parliament in Cairo, everybody shouts, jokes and pokes fun at each other.

A Saint's Birthday

Each January in an impoverished quarter of Cairo an exuberant celebration of a religious event takes place. It is the observance of the birthday of a beloved Muslim saint, Sidi 'Ali Zein el-'Abedin, a direct descendant of 'Ali, son-in-law of the Prophet Muhammed. Since the thirteenth century, Muslims in Cairo and other Middle Eastern cities have observed these *mulids*, or birthday feasts, celebrating the saints of Islam.[17]

Until a few years ago, virtually every quarter in each Egyptian town had its local saint. His tomb was revered and well tended, his memory venerated. The annual Muslim saints' birthday feasts are similar to religious festival celebrations of saints' days in Europe. On the final evening of the ten-day celebration, a long religious procession takes place and participants sometimes carry religious artifacts through the streets. In the *mulid* which occurs in Luxor in honor of Sheikh Abu Hajjaj, replicas of ancient barques, remnants of an ancient pagan rite, are paraded through town in a ceremonial procession.

The scene of the *mulid* in Cairo is the Sayyida Zeinab section, site of many once elegant houses built in the late medieval period. Now, at the end of the twentieth century, Sayyida Zeinab has fallen on hard times. The elegant, four-story houses, many still embellished with elaborately carved lattice-work windows, have become the slum dwellings of a fast-growing, high density population of mainly displaced and very poor peasants from the Nile Valley. The principal industry of the neighborhood consists of a large slaughterhouse. Near this abattoir is the nineteenth-century mosque of 'Ali Zein el-'Abedin, which was built over the site where this eighth-century figure of Islam is said to be buried. On any given day, flocks of sheep and herds of camels stained with vivid pink spray paint marking them for slaughter, are driven into a large cul-du-sac where the abattoir is located. These innocent creatures trot blithely to their impending execution. After the slaughter, the furs, hides, and wool are saved and various remaining parts are sent to glue factories, canneries, and butcher shops. Slaughter day is Wednesday and on this day, scores of butchers stand on the streets in their small shops, their hands and aprons drenched in blood and entrails.

Our drive to the *mulid* brought us through narrow streets reeking with a blend of open sewers and animal carcasses from the nearby butcher shops. We turned a corner and there before us was a heavily appliquéd funeral tent full of male mourners sitting in chairs, all visible to passersby as if on stage. Close by, at a large open square next to a mosque, we descended into the middle of a small traveling carnival. I saw tables full of pink sugar dolls and blue sugar horses, small boat rides, chariot swings for children and booths selling fringed paper hats. At booths offering air-rifle practice, the targets were plump kewpie dolls or photographs of glamorous female Egyptian movie stars. Trailers set up near the rides offered, for a small entrance fee, belly dancing, and Punch and Judy shows in which the audience always gets to see a shrewish wife beating her weak and ineffectual husband with a broomstick. Another trailer offered its patrons rapid circumcisions. Circumcisions performed on saints' birthdays are believed to endow the male child with a special blessing.

There is a proverb that says "No one leaves a *mulid* without hummus," the popular Middle Eastern grain. The grain has a religious significance. At every Egyptian saint's birth feast, bags of hummus are sold by the kilo. Each bag of grain is intended to feed the families of the followers of the saint. Thus, as the grain is consumed, the blessings of the saint will be spread into the community. Another concoction which is commonly sold outside *mulids* is a traditional Egyptian version of a Bloody Mary (minus the vodka). It consists of tomato juice, pepper, and hummus.

In search of the *mulid* itself, I followed the sound of flutes and unfamiliar musical incantations. This led me down a dark and covered alley which twisted and turned and seemed to have no end. On either side of this lane, Egyptian men sat engrossed in games of backgammon. All of them were pulling smoke from exotically shaped waterpipes and drinking glasses of sweet tea. I felt uneasy in this poor neighborhood, uncomfortably out of place and vulnerable. The alley ended, and suddenly I was in another huge appliquéd tent covered with red, green, and black geometric designs, all supported by tall wooden poles from which hung strings of multi-colored electric lights. Inside, the tent was warmed by the glow of a thousand lanterns.

In a large open area covered with prayer mats I watched the gyrating figures of a hundred or more Muslim women and men, all swaying from side to side and turning in half circles. A bandstand had been erected at one end of the dancing area. Musicians stood blowing flutes and recorders, and shaking jangling tambourines. On the bandstand was a man gripping a microphone. He half sang and half chanted a strange musical, rhythmic incantation. Later I was told that his words were full of the sensual imagery of romantic poetry, and constituted a popular hymn addressed to the Prophet. The music was pulsating with an exotic beat. The dancers were performing a *zikr,* some bending backward and forward, nodding their heads and again and again speaking the name of Allah. One man had an open safety pin stuck through the flesh on his left cheek. It did not bleed and he seemed to feel no pain. The figures continued to twist, turn, sway, dip and bend. Some of them reeled and then collapsed on the ground in an ecstatic trance. One fallen dancer fainted dead away and had to be carried off the tent floor.

Dark as the inner recesses of the tent were, I began to make out the shapes of tombstones. It became clear to me that I was standing in a graveyard. Egyptians are dedicated visitors to the graves of dead relatives. Part of the visiting ceremony involves distributing cakes or bread to the poor. It is believed that giving food to the living poor will speed the souls of the departed to heaven. The large tent was erected over many gravestones and mausoleums, all painted green, the color of the Prophet. The sides of the tent were tied to the gravestones. Smaller tents had been erected throughout the graveyard to house visitors to the *mulid* who came from long distances and represented different religious orders.

An old woman wrapped in black stood on a nearby tombstone and seemed to be guarding it. Almost as if she had been waiting for my arrival, she dropped down off the gravestone and motioned me to sit down. The old woman had offered me her family tomb as a viewing stand and from here I had a ringside view of the whirling dancers. I thanked her as best I could and gave her grandchild who stood nearby some hard candy and plastic barrettes.

On the edge of the dancing area were families and children of all ages who had come to watch. They clapped in time with the beat. With the rhythm of their applause, they followed the leader's signal for the dancers to change direction. The dancers now bent backward and forward and then whirled and jerked their heads. The pulsating musical accompaniment grew louder and faster and the leader sang with increased exuberance. Suddenly the music stopped. The dancers slowed their whirling frenzy. Several collapsed on the tent floor. Others walked away to take a cup of restorative hot tea. Yet, among the spectators, there was a universal spirit of serenity and well-being. Members of the audience now came up and smiled at me; some touched my sleeve as if for luck. They seemed pleased to have a Western stranger in their midst. When the musicians reassembled on the bandstand, the lead singer chanted in Arabic over the loudspeaker, "Welcome to the American lady with the camera."

Behind the bandstand, inside a small green mausoleum no more than nine feet square, a Muslim family was watching the performance and drinking tea. On another nearby gravestone, a second family had set up camp in the cemetery for the ten days of the pre-*mulid* celebration. Stirring a large pot, the wife was cooking dinner on a portable burner.

What I had witnessed was a traditional Sufi celebration of a saint's birthday. Sufism is a form of Islamic mysticism, a striving for spiritual purity. A Sufi renounces individual will. In twirling or performing the *zikr* in the *mulid* celebration, the Sufi is achieving oneness with God and strives towards a direct linkage with the Almighty. People come from all over Egypt to attend certain of the most important birthfeasts. A famous *mulid* in the Nile Delta at Tanta attracts over a million Egyptians each year. In an ecumenical feasting which takes place each year in Upper Egypt, Christians and Muslims regularly celebrate each other's saints.

I left the *mulid* with a small bag of Egyptian grain, a reminder that the blessings of the saint would spread goodness and well-being throughout Cairo.

This garlic seller offers the preferred seasoning for cooking in the Middle East. ▷
Garlic is believed to be both an aphrodisiac and a cure for impotence. Some
folk say it cures sixty different complaints. In the past, incisions were made in
rheumatic legs. Each day, garlic was rubbed into the open cuts. Pus flowed
from the wounds and, in time, the lame person got up and walked—possibly
to escape future garlic applications.

Overleaf: Shown here in Sayyida Zeinab, a poor quarter of Cairo, are members ▷▷
of a local Sufi cult rehearsing for the Mulid (birth feast) of Sidi 'Ali Zein
el-'Abedin. A major figure of Shi'ite Islam, this saint was a direct descendent
of 'Ali, son-in-law of the Prophet Muhammed. The celebration, a folk religious tradition, takes place in a Muslim graveyard among the tombs.

Sufism is a form of Islamic mysticism, a striving for spiritual purity. ''Sufi''
means ''wool'' and derives from the punishing, heavy wool cloaks worn in
hot weather, much like the hair shirts of medieval monks. Inspired by the
Prophet's life, Sufism stresses the values of austerity, poverty and rejection of
worldly things. In both the ascetic and humanistic form of Islam, the mystical
Sufis follow what they call the *Tariqa,* or Path. Sufis divide the Path into three
movements: purification, sacrifice, and knowledge. The Sufi who attains the
highest or final degree on the Path is called ''the knower of God.'' The image
of the difficult Path is a metaphor used by mystics in all the great world
religions.

While some Islamic scholars contend that Sufism is a legitimate form of
worship, Sufis have been accused of ''unorthodoxy'' and are disapproved of
in mainstream Islam. The *ulema,* orthodox Muslim scholars, strongly disap-
prove of the ''pagan excesses'' of the Sufis.

Sporting Ray-Bans and a turban, this urbane citizen of Cairo perched next to his bicycle, is a sartorial embodiment of east and west.

As an elderly woman, this Cairene moves freely in public without the permission of a male family member. ▷
Woven into the fabric of her headcloth is the traditional Islamic motif of the crescent moon and star.

◁ One of the mausoleums belonging to the fifteenth-century complex of the Sultan
  Barsbay may be seen through a crumbling stone wall. Intricately decorated with
  geometric, interlacing carvings, the dome covers a burial chamber.

This beautiful Cairene woman lives in a dwelling built on the city dump at Fustat. She works for a pottery-making family. If an Egyptian wife works, her income is her own and not her husband's.

Cairo's huge quantities of refuse are collected by the *zabbaliin,* a caste of garbage collectors. Cairo has recently banned the ▷ "unsightly" donkey carts, and trucks or tractors are used instead. These men are driving their trucks through the great cemetery of northern Cairo, past a domed complex of fifteenth-century tombs.

◁◁ *Previous page:* Child laborers are an all-too-familiar sight in Egypt. Wages for children are between a quarter and a third of those paid to adults. In the Egyptian countryside, children work in the fields alongside their parents as they have for centuries. To have only a few children or to be childless is considered a tragedy.

This Cairo girl's family produces water jars and other earthenware vessels. The family's kilns and dwellings are found side by side at the Cairo city dump in Fustat. A prosperous residential area during the Middle Ages, Fustat was torched by the Egyptians to prevent its capture by the armies of the Crusaders.

All ages work together at the pottery. Shown here are pots in the process of drying, ready to be fired. The kilns are fired with refuse from the dump, a cheap and productive way to recycle a small part of the tons of garbage generated every day in Cairo.

The crude, wooden walkway crosses a dry moat (now covered with a few inches of water—thanks to Cairo's inadequate sewage system). The walkway leads to the entrance of an eleventh-century keep which is built into the walls of medieval Cairo, near Bab al-Futuh (the "Gate of the Conquests"), the main northern gate of the city. Interior steps cut into the massive stone walls of the keep lead to crenellated ramparts. Inside the walls are tunnels and vast interrogation halls where enormous iron rings were hammered into the stones to hold manacled prisoners, all menacingly reminiscent of the Tower of London. The walls were thick enough to garrison many hundreds of troops in huge, vaulted chambers. The walls connect Bab al-Futuh with the other northern gate, the Bab al-Nasr (Gate of Victory). Perhaps because of the walls, Cairo was never besieged.

The wheels of this Egyptian cart evoke images of ancient Roman chariots. The driver passes Bab ▷
al-Nasr ("The Gate of Victory"), the easternmost of the two northern gates of medieval Cairo.

A sister and brother in Old Cairo have been feeding a tethered sheep brought into the city for slaughter. The animal will be the main course at the "Great Feast of the Sacrifice" which takes place sixty days after the fast of Ramadan, the Muslim month of atonement. Ramadan marks the month when, thirteen centuries ago, the Prophet Muhammed began to receive the divine word of God. Observance of Ramadan is one of the five religious duties required of a faithful Muslim.

In Old Cairo, an Egyptian wife contemplates a painting on the facade of her house memorializing her husband's *Hajj,* or pilgrimage to the Holy Mosque in Mecca. As the wall painting graphically illustrates, her mate completed the journey both by boat and airplane.

On a holiday outing, Egyptian schoolgirls pass the elaborate, domed fountain which is located in the center of the courtyard of the Mosque, the *madrasa* of Sultan Hasan. A *madrasa* was a center for the study of Islamic law. The building was completed about 1360 A.D., although the central fountain was added some three centuries later.

The poor in Cairo often live amid the elegance of a bygone era. Once the four-story home of a wealthy ▷ Cairo family, this nineteenth-century building now houses poor families who often live five or six persons to a room.

From the thirteenth to the seventeenth centuries, delicate screens and covered windows of intricately carved, wooden lattice work were characteristic of the most luxurious private houses. In the *mashrabiyya* alcoves behind the windows, water in porous, earthen bottles evaporated to provide an early mode of air conditioning. Sometimes almost touching each other, these projecting windows hung out over the narrow streets of Cairo. As an elegant touch, the builder frequently added arabesque reliefs and small pieces of colored glass set in wooden frames. The *hareem,* or part of the house designated for women, was required to be as secluded and private as possible. No outsider's eyes were permitted to gaze upon the cloistered womenfolk, who rarely left their protected spaces.

Near the Coptic Museum in Old Cairo, a young fruit and vegetable seller stops to rest. Her black overdress shows that she is married.

◁ This man works at a traditional spinning wheel. He has moved from a village in Upper Egypt to try his luck in Cairo's northern cemetery, the City of the Dead.

The population of Cairo increases by one person every ninety seconds and housing shortages are severe. More than half a million new arrivals, *fellahin* from rural villages desperately searching for a better life, have moved permanently into the cemetery where they have set up households and business establishments between the mosques and gravestones. There is even a videotape store in this huge, urban burial ground. However, business does not seem to be flourishing.

Situated in Cairo's beautiful northern cemetery known as the City of the Dead, these graceful domes ornament the tomb-mosques of the Mamluk sultans.

Cairo, ruled by the Mamluk sultans from the thirteenth to the sixteenth centuries, was the greatest city in the Middle East and the glory of Islam. It was a city of *A Thousand and One Nights.* The Mamluk sultans drove the Crusaders back to the sea and the Mongols back to the steppes.

51

Perhaps the most familiar landmark in Cairo, the richly appointed, alabaster Muhammed 'Ali Mosque stands near the twelfth-century walls of the Citadel of Cairo. Constructed on the site of the 'Ayyubid Palace where, in 1219, St. Francis of Assisi preached to the Sultan al-Kamil, the Mosque is notable for its slender minarets and Byzantine-style domes. Inspired by the Hagia Sophia in Istanbul, it was begun in 1824 A.D. by the great Egyptian liberator, Muhammed 'Ali, and completed in 1857 under his successor, Said.

The Citadel itself was conceived by Saladin, the twelfth-century Muslim warrior and the nemesis of Richard the Lion-Hearted and other Crusaders. A Kurd by birth, Saladin waged successful military campaigns in North Africa, Nubia, Palestine, Western Arabia and Central Syria, ultimately bringing these territories under his control. He returned victorious to Cairo, where he conceived the idea of creating an impregnable city. The defensive ring of walls around Cairo was completed by thousands of Crusader prisoners.

◁ This Cairo woman stands in front of a nineteenth-century *sabil. Sabils,* or water fountains, were endowed by wealthy Muslims to provide free drinking water for all the townspeople.

Male family members carry the body of a relative across the courtyard of the ▷ funerary complex of the Mamluk sultan, Faraj ibn Barquq. The corpse is wrapped in green, the color of the Prophet. The evening before, a wake will have been held by the family. After verses of the *Qur'an* have been read, the body will be carried out for burial. On the way to the cemetery, the somber procession will be joined by passersby, some of whom may be total strangers. Nevertheless, out of reverence and piety, they will participate, even helping to carry the body for a short distance.

The funerary complex of Faraj ibn Barquq was completed about 1410 A.D. It includes an enormous *khanqah* (a center for Sufi studies and practices) consisting of a central courtyard surrounded by arcades and residential quarters. The eastern side of the building is notable for its large, arcaded prayer area, flanked by two domed burial chambers. Built entirely of stone, the carved chevron pattern which decorates the exterior of the building is a remarkable feat of Mamluk design. Pictured here is the south dome which covers the burial chambers of Shiriz and Shakra, sisters of the builder. The north dome, not pictured, houses the tomb chamber in which Faraj and his father, the Sultan Barquq, are buried.

◁◁ *Previous page:* After the burial of a loved one, Egyptian families of all income levels rent mourning tents appliquéd in brilliant colors. Wakes are attended by men only. Visitors sip cups of unsweetened black coffee, a symbol of grief and sorrow. Verses are read from the *Qur'an.* The neon letters in the sign spell ''Allah.''

Overleaf: At noon on Friday, the Muslim Sabbath, thousands of the faithful gather for prayers at al-Husayn Mosque in Cairo. The Mosque quickly fills to overflowing and thousands more crowd into the enormous, open square outside.

Egypt's most distinguished contemporary writer, Naguib Mahfouz, described the scene:

''The call to prayer was given. The men rose all at once and positioned themselves in closely packed lines which filled the courtyard of the great mosque. They brought the building to life with their bodies and souls. . . . Intermingled in the long, parallel lines were men with all different styles of clothing—suits, cloaks, or floor-length shirts—but they all become a single organism, moving in unison, facing in a single direction for prayer. Their whispered recitations reverberated in an all-encompassing hum until the benediction came.''

◁ This woman sits on a bench at Bayt al-Suhaymi, a restored merchant's house of late medieval Cairo. Her black outer dress and simple hair covering are typical of poor Muslim women living in Cairo.

Overleaf: The scene is the lively Friday camel market at Imbaba outside of Cairo. What ▷▷ seems at first to be a peculiar, lurching, three-legged beast is, in fact, a normal, four-legged camel hobbled with rope to keep him from running away or wreaking havoc among the vendors of harnesses, rope, saddles, camel blankets, sheep and goats.

The Imbaba market is the largest in the Middle East. Camels come from as far away as Somalia, Arabia, and the Sudan. In the crowd of dark-skinned men, one can identify the Somali cameleers who often wear leopard-skin slippers and carry sharp daggers in sheaths ornamented with leopard fur. Pampered and fed with the finest clover, camels from Somalia command the highest prices, up to $2,000. These "best of show" animals are so valuable that they make the 2,000 mile trip by truck. Such prize animals will not be sold for meat but will be used for fine breeding. Somali camels are distinguished by their velvety, dark eyes and a flawless muscular contour. They are far superior to the bony animals shown here, which are headed for slaughter. The choice camels serenely watch the melée of groaning, grumpy Sudanese beasts being whipped by their drivers.

The Sudanese camel drivers travel nine hundred miles from Western Sudan to Imbaba, a grueling, forty-day journey, crossing the desert on foot to Khartoum, and eventually reaching Aswan and a railroad running to Cairo. The going is not without hazards. Traveling from well to well, some camels may stray from the caravan, hunting for hashish which, in the words of the nineteenth-century explorer, Arthur Silva White "they sidle up to with the stealthy tread of a villain in a melodrama." Along the long march to Imbaba, camels may stray from the herd, die of thirst, drop from exhaustion, or be stolen in an ambush by desert raiders.

Camel meat is sold all over Egypt. A large Sudanese camel may yield 700 pounds of meat at a dollar a pound. Camel meat costs two-thirds the price of lamb or beef, making it more affordable to poorer Egyptians who often eat little more than beans and bread. The younger camels are purchased by subsistence farmers for transporting sugar cane, grain, fodder, and other agricultural produce in rural areas of the Nile Delta or Upper Egypt. At Imbaba, a healthy, young camel, destined to be a beast of burden, will sell for U.S. $350. To determine the camel's age a buyer will always insist on examining its teeth. The shorn, silky camel hair is a renewable source of income for camel owners and will end up in expensive coats sold in the finest shops in Rome, Paris, and New York.

Cameleers find time to gossip, enjoy
their waterpipes of sweet-smelling
tobacco and buy cups of strong, black
tea. Makeshift teahouses like this one
are common at the Friday camel market
at Imbaba, a suburb of Cairo.

The attire of this lounger at a railroad crossing in Old Cairo includes a Jordanian scarf
and high-heeled, western loafers.

Throughout Egypt, the mark of a right hand dipped in animal blood appears on walls and above doorways. It ▷
even shows up on jewelry and on harnesses of horses. Called "The Hand of Fatima," the mark is believed to be a
magical symbol of strength and a protection against the pervasive Evil Eye.

Sometimes the mark was made by dipping the hand in the blood of a sacrificial goat or sheep. In Muslim
tradition, the right hand is pure, the left, unclean. Food is always eaten with the right hand. Offering the left hand
to a friend or stranger is an unacceptable affront.

◁◁ *Previous page:* Waiting for the chaotic bargaining to begin at Imbaba's camel market, these leathery-skinned,
Sudanese cameleers rest after their forty-day journey. A middleman physically stands between the traders,
helping them to make a deal and literally pushing the two negotiators together. The brokers are well paid for their
skills. Kibitzers stand on the sidelines making unkind remarks about the pitiful condition of the camels.

Sinai

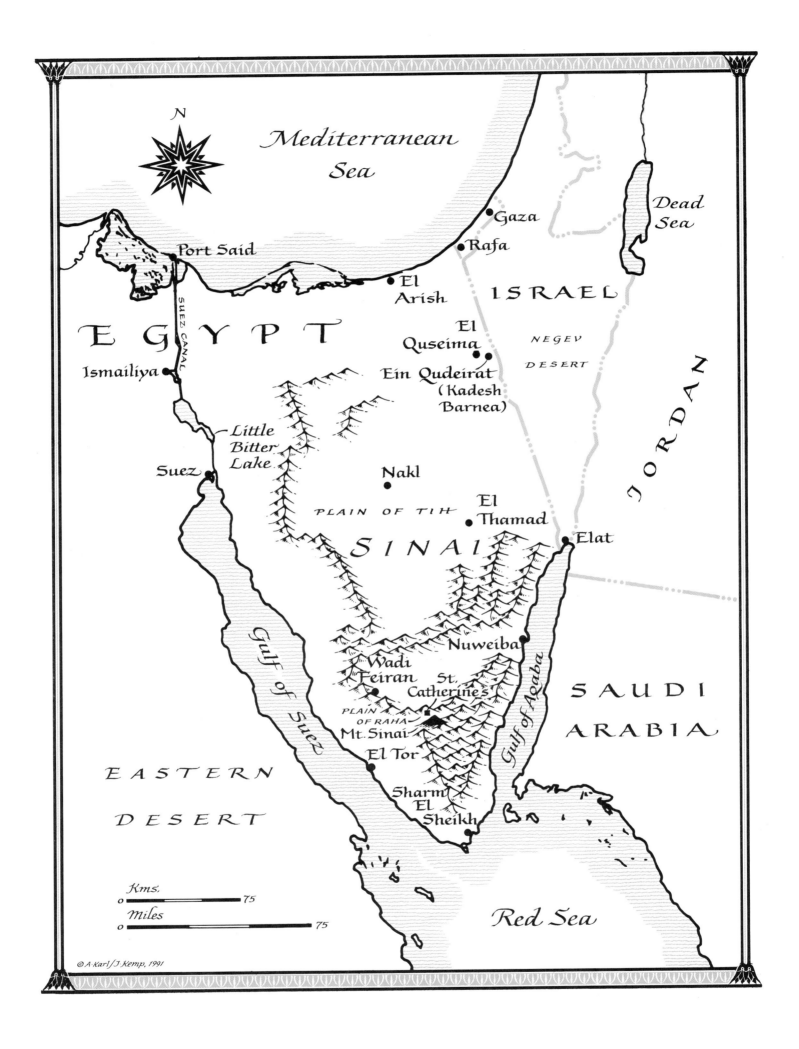

© A·Karl/J·Kemp, 1991

Sinai

East to the Great Wilderness

On January 2nd, 1990, I left New York City on my fourth trip to Egypt, this time to study and document the Bedouin tribes of the Sinai peninsula. The next day, my plane touched down at Cairo's Heliopolis Airport. I headed immediately for the American Embassy to keep an appointment with the U.S. Ambassador, Frank Wisner. It was a busy time for the Embassy. Visiting congressmen on junkets, ostensibly there to study the U.S. Foreign Aid Mission, were arriving in droves, expecting red carpet treatment and personal, customized tours of the city.

Part of a heavily defended and walled military compound situated in central Cairo, the American Embassy's elaborate security measures operate day and night. After passport and permit clearance by a phalanx of armed Egyptian and U.S. military personnel, an official Embassy pass hanging from my neck, I was escorted across a huge courtyard into the Embassy building itself. Ambassador Wisner is a broad-shouldered man of medium height who exudes charm, power and a clear sense of what he wants to accomplish. He ushered me graciously into his cavernous office.

After affable inquiries into the well-being of mutual friends, the Ambassador became deadly serious. He advised me that he felt it essential that I be accompanied by an Egyptian military escort throughout Sinai. He brought his director of military security, Colonel Lemon (a gentleman who closely resembled a worried Humphrey Bogart), into the office to emphasize his point.

I was dismayed by this edict. On my 1989 trip to photograph oases and Arab nomads in the Western Desert, I found that Egyptian officials are regarded with suspicion among the Bedouin. I was certain that an entourage of Egyptian military men would preclude any ease or intimacy I might be able to establish with the desert people. The Ambassador and Colonel Lemon brushed aside my protests. I could do nothing to dissuade them. The Ambassador assured me that he was privy to classified information suggesting considerable risk in the remote areas of Sinai to which I would be traveling. Since I was planning to spend time near the Israeli border and had sought his protection, he was duty-bound to provide it. While disappointed by the verdict, I pushed ahead since photographs of Bedouin life were indispensable to my project. Ironically, it turned out that the military escort won me access to closed areas of the desert as well as an introduction to His Excellency, Munir Ahmad Muhammad Shash, Governor of North Sinai, and to many helpful academics, expert on Bedouin life and culture.

On a gray, rainy morning a few days later, we set out with our Egyptian driver, Samir Abu Bakr el Said, for the Sinai. Directly behind me in the minivan sat a lieutenant colonel on loan from the Egyptian military. He was to be my official escort as far as el-'Arish, capital of North Sinai, an easy, four-hour journey from Cairo.

The drive east from Cairo to Sinai begins with endless apartment-filled suburbs, many containing offices, housing and sports clubs for important members of the Egyptian military. The colonel pointed out his apartment. His windows were black rectangles in a sterile, tan tower. I pictured in my mind a visit to the colonel's home. On entering one would breathe in the lingering odor of Egyptian tobacco smoke. On the walls would hang a framed portrait of President Hosni Mubarak and a wedding picture of the colonel and his wife, she, clad in a pink satin wedding gown, smiling shyly. The furniture would be unpretentious and utilitarian. There would be a television, a tape player, and a VCR. The apartment would consist of a sitting room, a tiny kitchen with no dishwasher, a small bedroom for the colonel and his wife, one for his two young daughters, seven years old and eighteen months, and a miniscule cubicle for their three-year-old son whom the colonel, smiling broadly, declared to be "pharaoh" of the household.

The colonel solemnly chided me, making no effort to conceal his feelings that Sinai Bedouin are unworthy subjects for me. Surely my plan to photograph Bedouin women was an enormous waste of time. Far better for me to travel directly to the Egyptian resort of Sharm el-Sheikh on Sinai's southernmost tip, where I could photograph "beautiful high rise hotels filled with snorkelers and scuba divers." My protestations that Bedouin are a dying part of indigenous Arab culture failed to move him. It was clear that little love is lost between the Bedouin and the Egyptian authorities. To change the subject, I asked him to teach me a few words in Arabic. We began with *maalesh.* It means "too bad" or "don't let it bother you" and is usually spoken with a shrug, often by a Cairene cyclist who has just ridden over your toe.

My mind turned back to the road to Sinai. We were proceeding east along the same highway which, three weeks later in early February, 1990, would be the site of the internationally publicized terrorist bomb attack on a bus full of Israeli tourists. In hindsight, I wondered what possible protection the colonel might have provided if we had been near the explosion when it occurred. After a two-hour drive, we stopped at the large Egyptian city of Ismailiya (population 450,000) to obtain a pass for the Suez Canal crossing.

The dream of establishing a waterway connecting the Red Sea to the Mediterranean goes back three thousand years. Ramses II did part of the job in 1280 B.C. Six hundred years later, in the Twenty-Sixth Dynasty, King Necho produced a second extension of the canal. In a later effort, according to Herodotus, work was abandoned not because it had cost the lives of 100,000 workers but because an oracle had detected unfavorable omens. Later, Persian engineers working under Darius I, and later still, Emperor Trajan during the Roman period, built and rebuilt the canal only to have it silt in and disappear under the desert sands. In the most successful engineering feat of the nineteenth century, the present canal was completed by the Suez Canal Company in 1869.

About six kilometers from Ismailiya, we arrived at the canal. Here we boarded a ferry boat large enough to carry five cars and one truck loaded with soft drinks. As our small ferry crossed the still, brown canal waters, we saw an enormous oil tanker headed north, flying the Liberian flag. Except for the scale of the tanker, the crossing seemed no more remarkable than one over a tributary of the Delaware River. But great excitement lay ahead. It was mid-January. The desert was waking up. The birds had migrated south across the Mediterranean. The implacable sun of the summer months had softened. The Bedouin tribesmen were returning to greening pastures. Fabled Sinai lay before us.

The wedge-shaped Sinai peninsula with its burning sands and pink granite rock sits at the crossroads of Africa and the Middle East. A backdrop for many of the legendary miracles of the Old Testament, the Sinai is described in the Book of Deuteronomy as "a great and terrible wilderness." According to biblical tradition, it was in Sinai that the Egyptian soldiers found Abraham and gave him gifts before sending him home, and here that God appeared to the prophet Moses and spoke to him from the Burning Bush. Later, on Mount Sinai, a thundering God gave the Ten Commandments to Moses. At Little Bitter Lake in Northwestern Sinai under the reign of Ramses II, the Lord swept back the waters of the Red Sea in 1250 B.C., permitting the children of Israel to escape the war chariots of the Pharaoh. Thirteen hundred years later, Mary and Joseph, carrying the baby Jesus, crossed and recrossed the Sinai from Egypt to Palestine, frustrating the edict of King Herod of Judea. In Judeo-Christian traditions, the Wandering in the Wilderness and the Exodus of the Jews from Egypt across the Plain of el-Raha, took place in the Sinai, on this barren land bridge that separates Africa from Asia.

The Sinai was formed over a million years ago. One thousand square miles of sedimentary rock were scraped and blasted over the millenia by massive, prehistoric storms and earthquakes. Brilliantly colored cliffs of iron and manganese were left behind. From the First Dynasty in 3000 B.C. through the Twenty-First Dynasty in 1100 B.C., the Egyptian pharaohs mined the copper and turquoise deposits of the Sinai. To its eternal grief, Sinai has been the gateway to Egypt and Africa since it must be crossed by invaders moving either toward Africa or the Middle East. From earliest times, probably dating to the Bronze Age (5000 B.C.), the Sinai has been a land of strife. Over thirty or more centuries, it has been the battleground of the armies of Babylon, Egypt, Greece, Rome, Syria, Persia, France, and England. Invading Ottomans, Hittites, Egyptians, Assyrians, Christians, Hebrews, Bedouin and Mamluks have all had their day advancing or retreating over the strategic military highways of the Sinai peninsula.

The modern history of Sinai begins with the break-up of the Ottoman Empire in the late nineteenth century and the opening of the Suez Canal in 1869. By the turn of the century, the British Empire had a firm hold on the Suez Canal, the Gulf of Suez, the Red Sea and the Gulf of 'Aqaba. After World War II, control of Sinai was ceded to Egypt while England retained her mandate over Palestine. This arrangement came to a close with the founding of the State of Israel in 1948. In the intervening years, the sacred sands of Sinai and its strategic neighboring Gaza Strip have been the sites of endless wrangling, crises, wars, and bloodbaths. Israel captured Sinai in 1967 but returned it to Egypt in the Camp David Treaty of 1979. Although divided into three security zones occupied by multinational peacekeeping forces and observers, Egypt was once again in sole possession of Sinai by 1982. Through all the devastation the real proprietors remain, the Bedouin pursuing their nomadic ways, a people that many anthropologists date to the early Bronze Age.

The Bedouin Tribes of North Sinai

The Arabic word *badawi* means "dweller of the desert." In modern usage, anyone who rears sheep or camels and who lives in a tent in an African or Middle Eastern desert is generally called a Bedouin. But in a more technical sense, the term "Bedouin" refers to the descendants of an ancient tribe of sheep- and camel-rearing nomads who, thousands of years ago, migrated north from Yemen and the southwestern quarter of the Arabian peninsula into the deserts of northern Africa and the Middle East. In a broader view, the Bedouin are indigenous Arabs identified mainly for their seminal role in Arab history. In his *The Arabs in History*, Bernard Lewis writes:

> For Muhammed and his contemporaries the Arabs were the Bedouin of the desert, and in the Qur'an the term is used exclusively in this sense and never of the townsfolk of Mecca, Medina and other cities . . . the purest form of Arabic is that of the Bedouin who have preserved more faithfully than any others the original Arab way of life and speech . . . The dominant feature of the population of central and northern Arabia in this crucial period before the rise of Islam is Bedouin tribalism.[1]

Almost all scholars confirm the role of the Bedouin as central to Arab culture and origins. The noted American biblical scholar, William Foxwell Albright, wrote "The Bedouin are the heirs of over thirty centuries of camel-nomadism and of some thirteen centuries of Islam."[2]

Throughout the Middle East, the Bedouin are organized into patriarchal kinship groups originally made up of fathers, sons, and their families. These tribes are further divided into clans as distinctive as the Scottish highlanders. All Bedouin of North Sinai have tribal affiliations. Among Bedouin, as in the rest of Egypt, marriages of first cousins are common, the preferable match being to marry one's father's niece or nephew. This system of frequent marriages between first and second cousins makes for a large and complicated blood-related group which will band together in defense of tribal interests. Individuality is discouraged as loyalties are directed to the tribe or clan, which in turn assumes responsibility or blame for the behavior of members. And, when an individual member is wronged, vengeance or reparation is always a tribal responsibility. That mission is carried out by the tribal sheikh, or chief.

As in most societies, there are outcasts. Second-class tribes are called *hatim,* disdained because they are not pure Arabian. In North Sinai, the members of the Akarsa tribe are believed to have descended from some of Napoleon's soldiers who fathered children of Bedouin when they came to Egypt at the very end of the eighteenth century. By custom, the Akarsa are not allowed to intermarry with members of pure Arabian tribes. The Jebeliya of South Sinai may have a far more venerable lineage but still have outcast status. They are descendants of slaves of the Emperor Justinian who were sent in the sixth century to protect the monks of St. Catherine's Monastery. A few Jebeliya have blond hair and blue eyes. No self-respecting Sinai tribesman will marry a Jebeliya.

Legends passed down through generations ensure that outcast tribes stay that way. One story goes, for example, that in the time of the Prophet Muhammed, a grandmother in the Dowagra tribe of North Sinai was given a written message by the Prophet. He ordered her to hide the message in her hair. The old woman betrayed the Prophet by giving the message to his enemies. Although most scholars agree that Muhammed couldn't write, after fourteen hundred years this story is still regarded as gospel and, accordingly, the Dowagra are regarded as inferior. To marry a member of the Dowagra tribe would bring shame upon the family of a "pure Arabian tribe." While not formally established, these traditions are as firmly entrenched as codified law.

The western world superficially defines the Bedouin by their tents, camels, and their endless transit of the desert sands. But a Bedouin will tell you that to be a Bedouin is to abide by a complex and often heroic code of behavior. These rules solidify a powerful sense of family and tribal unity. They encompass a passion for justice or vengeance, especially as it affects the family or clan, pride in acts of manhood, patience in the face of adversity, and bravery, frequently to the point of preferring death over shame or public humiliation. The old Arab saying goes, "life without honor is nothing," and "life without justice is not worth living." While proud, disciplined and fearless, the Bedouin are also profoundly religious Muslims with a deep sense of sexual modesty and propriety. It is these qualities that were so admired by Victorians and romanticized by Hollywood.

Today, governments and city dwellers in many Third World countries view desert nomadism as a major obstacle to economic development. Accordingly, scholars of pastoral societies often are responsible for many of the negative stereotypes about Bedouin cultural values and lifestyles. Even in the minds of many urban Egyptians and westerners, the romantic image of the burnoose-covered head, the powerful, Semitic face, and the flowing, white robes belted with a sword or dagger has given way to feelings of suspicion or loathing. According to the American scholar, Dr. Joseph Hobbs, a distinguished authority on Bedouin culture, "Nile-dwellers have always been more fearful than enchanted of the Egyptian desert. The ancient Egyptians classified their terrestrial world into good and bad lands: the benevolent black land, named for the fecund black soil of the Nile Valley, and the unyielding red land of desert rock and sand."[3] For centuries, the desert people of Sinai have been regarded by Cairenes and Nile villagers as gypsies, thieves, smugglers and persons of low intelligence.

T.E. Lawrence, immortalized as Lawrence of Arabia, romanticized the Bedouin and he wrote idealistically of the desert nomads with whom he had broken bread, dressed in the robes of a Bedouin sheikh. But his feelings were both ambivalent and colonialist. In *The Seven Pillars of Wisdom,* he wrote in 1920 that the Bedouin are:

a limited narrow-minded people whose inert intellects lie uncuriously fallow . . . They invent no systems of philosophy or mythologies . . . Their convictions are by instinct, their activities intuitional . . . They know only truth and untruth, belief and unbelief, without our hesitating retinue of finer shades . . . [the Bedouin] enjoys the little vices and luxuries—coffee, fresh water, women—which he can still afford . . . There follows a self-delight in pain, a cruelty which is more to him than goods. The desert Arab finds no joy like the joy of voluntarily holding back. He finds luxury in abnegation, renunciation, self-restraint. He lives his own life in hard selfishness. His desert is made a spiritual ice-house, in which is preserved intact but unimproved for all ages an idea of the unity of God.[4]

Equally biased, the ancient Egyptians referred to the desert tribes as "sand fleas."[5] In his book, *Sinai: The Great and Terrible Wilderness,* Burton Bernstein notes that in the fourteenth century, a famous Arab historian named ibn Khaldun derided the Bedouin as unmanageable and ignorant nomads—"the most savage human beings that exist . . . on a level with wild untamable animals and dumb beasts of prey."[6]

The Bedouin today still believe that a settled life signifies a loss of freedom. They endure the cruelties of life in the desert that they may follow their passion for sleeping under the beauty of the stars. They delight in telling stories about people who have traveled to the Nile Valley to visit relatives only to sicken and die. Life in the towns, they feel, is corrupt and polluted while life in the desert is clean and pure. The Bedouin see themselves as an impoverished nobility, not as poor relations, barely surviving in the wilderness. Above all, they are fiercely devoted to their *naqwa,* the ancient Bedouin code of honor, in which one endures extreme hunger in order to feed a kinsman.

From the beginning of camel domestication in the Arabian desert in the second millenium B.C., the desert Arabs have guided their lives according to a variety of beliefs and astrological commands. For example, according to Joseph Hobbs, there are both propitious and unfavorable days for travel: "The second day of the second lunar month is favorable. The nineteenth day of any lunar month is favorable. The worst days are the three of *al-Giraan,* the conjunction of the moon with the constellation Scorpio (*al-Agrab*) and Thursdays (*yawm al-Khamiis*) which fall on the twenty-fifth day of the Muslim lunar month." During unlucky astrological periods, the Bedouin may not engage in sexual intercourse as a baby born at the wrong time might be retarded.[7]

According to Edward H. Palmer, the nineteenth-century scholar of the Sinai, the Bedouin believe that when a man rises in the morning, the spirit of God sits upon his right shoulder and the devil on his left. The man must sprinkle himself with water and say "I seek refuge in God from Satan accursed with stones." Without this precaution, the devil will be with him all day.[8] Palmer also writes that Bedouin believe God first created man and then gave him camels, goats, asses and donkeys for his use along with time and seasons.[9] Travelers in Sinai still notice on Bedouin tents a little bundle of charms hung on one of the tent poles to avert the Evil Eye. I saw one such collection consisting of a black cock's leg, a red rag, a dried frog, two bones, and a little leather charm, tied together and hung on the pole. In common with many Egyptians, Bedouin believe in *jinn,* invisible spirits who live under the ground. *Jinn* may be heard in "the howling wind and the singing sands." Like young American men, the Bedouin have superstitions which, when faithfully observed, will win the love of a woman. Palmer describes a Bedouin tradition in which a tribesman takes the body of a vulture, buries it for forty days and then boils the body in water until all the flesh has disappeared. The first white bone that sticks up out of the pot is a love charm. If you rub it on the dress of a girl, you instantly secure her affections.[10]

While Bedouin will obediently line up for innoculations from visiting doctors, they also believe in the miraculous healing powers of "burned owl feathers and boiled hyena flesh."[11] Children wear charms and amulets around their necks both to frighten off the Evil Eye and to cure disease. A common Bedouin superstition is that boy babies should be breast fed longer than girls. It is believed that this indulgence will produce fearlessness as the boy grows older.

In Bedouin society, omens and superstitions have inferior rank to the commands of Islam. And the Islamic virtues of faith in God, self-sacrifice, daily prayer, patience, piety, and acts of charity are deeply imbedded in Bedouin culture. T.E. Lawrence observes: "There was a homeliness, an everydayness of this climatic Arab God, who was their eating and their fighting and their lusting . . . Each individual nomad has his revealed religion, not oral or traditional or expressed, but instinctive in himself . . . a stress on the emptiness of the world and the fullness of God."[12]

According to Joseph Hobbs, the Bedouin, although extremely devout, appear to other Muslims to be more lax in their rituals. Their nomadic pursuits in remote locations prevent them from attending mosque regularly. Yet, when the rooster crows each morning, male members of Bedouin camps still gather outside their tents and engage in the first of the five prescribed daily communal prayers. In addition to observing the five Muslim prayers of the day (or most of them) the Bedouin male usually adheres to alms giving, fasting during Ramadan and, if he can afford it, the *Hajj* or pilgrimage to Mecca at least once in his lifetime.

Unquestionably the ancient cults and superstitions of Bedouin society have been protected by illiteracy, tribalism and physical isolation. Memory and the oral traditions still predominate over writing. Although many Bedouin today prize literacy and education, it appears that, at best, only one out of every ten in Sinai can read or write. And when grade school education is available, most girls still lose out.

Probably the most durable and impressive feature of Bedouin culture is its unwritten legal system.[13] Standing rock firm against the influence of centuries of Ottoman, British, French, Egyptian and Israeli rule, the peninsula's Bedouin continue to live by their highly ceremonial and formulaic arbitration procedures for the resolution of disputes and the redress of wrongs.

In western culture, criminal law is usually rooted in deterrence. But as with many tribal folk, the law of the Bedouin is based on vengeance and reparations. Crimes such as rape, murder, trespass, theft or violation of the tent (the Bedouin counterpart of trespass) are regarded as insults to honor. Very frequently the need for reparations may be satisfied by the award of a set number of camels.

Premeditated murder is the gravest of offenses. In accordance with the tradition that recognizes tribal rather than individual responsibility for wrongs, the male cousins, *humsa,* of the victim are permitted to seek "blood vengeance" against the male relatives of the murderer. This may include execution, usually by a firing squad, the object being to restore a numerical balance between the families or tribes. However, any relative of the murderer may buy personal protection if he surrenders a camel six years old, or older (or its equivalent in money) to the kin of the deceased. This is known as the "camel of sleep" since the one who has surrendered it (and his sons) may sleep peacefully because they are no longer subject to retaliation. The injured family's pursuit of vengeance then proceeds against the male kin of the murderer who have not paid protection money. This, in turn, leads to the negotiation and payment of blood money by the kin of the murderer to the avenging kin of the deceased. The state of agitation prior to settlement is called the "boiling over of blood." During this presettlement period there prevails a singular custom under which the victim's family may take whatever movable belongings they come across belonging to the murderer, except for utensils for making coffee. In cases of deeply-rooted tribal feuds, settlement may be refused. In some Bedouin societies the killer may then be marked for death at the hands of the victim's kin.

Physical mutilation as a punishment for crime is still practiced among the Bedouin of Saudi Arabia, but among the Sinai Bedouin the draconian pronouncements calling for the mutilation of the body of the criminal are purely symbolic. For rape, for example, the nominal sentence may be "the penis is to be cut off or it may be ransomed with ten camels" or the verdict may be "the hand which touched her is to be cut off or it may be ransomed with ten camels." In one case there was judgment that "the eye that saw her is to be cut out but it may be ransomed with ten camels." In a second flip-flop, the award of camels was then converted into an equivalent in money. Yet the Bedouin desire for justice or vengeance has very little to do with financial gain. In the case of rape, the injured husband or father values most the judicial award of the white silk flag which is placed on a family tent as a sign that the woman remains unsullied.

The following offenses are unusually grave, and may be punished by a double or quadruple penalty: theft after trespassing upon an area where dates are dried; trespass over the inviolable boundaries of a Bedouin tent; falsely accusing a guarantor of not fulfilling his obligations ("cutting the face"); cursing the house of a tribesman; injury to a palm tree; and falsely accusing a woman of infidelity or stripping off her veil. In the desert, a most heinous crime and indignity is the affront of striking a man in the face with a shoe or sandal. No Bedouin would ever dream of saying "sticks and stones may break my bones but words will never hurt me."

Strict procedures are required to establish the guilt of an accused person. Two reliable witnesses are required. But ancient superstitions sometimes supersede rational inquiry. If guilt cannot be established, a "trial by fire", or *bash'a,* method of proof is still commonly used among Sinai Bedouin. The *bash'a,* a long-handled iron spoon used to roast coffee beans, is heated until it is red hot. The accused must swear to the truth of what he says—then he must lick the *bash'a* three times with his tongue. A *mubasha'* (judge of the *bash'a*), who, during the ordeal, always sits facing Mecca, examines the effect on the tongue. If the tongue shows a mark from the heat, the accused is guilty. No burn mark is certain proof that he is innocent. Professor Larry W. Roeder, Jr., a specialist in the *bash'a,* calls this procedure the "polygraph of fire."[14]

Hospitality is a sacred rule of the desert largely because lives depend on it. The Bedouin could not travel great distances to markets or grazing lands without the formalities of hospitality, which must be reciprocated. A stranger will be extended food and lodging for three days in a Bedouin camp. Under the code of the desert a Bedouin must allow even a mortal enemy to rest, eat and drink in his tent, after which he must be permitted to leave in peace. This reciprocal hospitality extends to sharing of resources. While all Bedouin tribes have well-defined grazing areas, they commonly permit other tribesmen to use these pastures. A sudden and unpredictable shower can produce instant growth of fodder. It is sound economic strategy to share this wealth and abundance with others. Who knows where the rain will fall next time?

Centuries-old wedding customs and rituals vary among the tribes. In many cases the bride has never met her groom before the wedding day and, in rare instances, has never seen him. But many Bedouin marriages are based on romantic love rather than family arrangements. An early account reported that a young man who wished to marry went to his intended's camp and sang his own plaintive verses to her. If the girl's family approved, the virgin's father sealed the contract by handing the bridegroom a green twig which he wrapped and carried in his turban for three days.

As a hedge against the unfortunate day when the groom might declare three times "I divorce you," the groom's family, after prolonged negotiations, puts up a dowry. The bridal wealth varies between two and twenty camels. In addition, the groom must provide a complete outfit of clothes for the bride, a carpet and a straw mat, a length of cloth to divide off the female quarters from the rest of the tent, cooking utensils, and a pair of heavy silver armlets. A copious bridal gift endows a woman with superior status—even lifetime prestige—enabling her to become a kind of chief woman of the camp. Bedouin brides are customarily led to the *birza* (wedding tent) on a decorated camel provided by the groom. The bride circles the tent three times, then dismounts and enters the tent with a female attendant. Here she remains. In another part of the Bedouin camp, the wedding banquet begins. Guests devour sheep killed for the occasion. After the feast and a celebration accompanied by great merriment among his male friends and relatives, the groom enters the tent, leaving his sandals outside, tears away the bride's face-covering and consummates the marriage.

Among the Muzeina tribe of South Sinai, it has been the custom for the bride to escape the wedding tent and attempt to hide in the mountains. If the bride finds the groom attractive, she may allow herself to be captured sooner than later. On the other hand, if the groom does not appeal to her, she may hide behind boulders for several days.

Muslim law permits four wives and in some parts of the Arab world, men have several wives whom they visit on a rotating basis. Sinai Bedouin seldom have more than one wife. But where the marriage, be it arranged or chosen, turns out to be a mistake, the men may escape through divorce or polygamous arrangements. To protect the patriarchal system's need for certainty about paternity, a divorced woman may not remarry until several menstrual periods have elapsed.

Possession of a few sheep, camels, goats, and some date or apricot trees is not enough to support a Bedouin family. Over the years, the Bedouin have become world-class smugglers and spies. Historically, they have never respected or recognized geographical and political barriers. Crossing a border on a camel in a remote desert area is not difficult for nomadic tribesmen. Unencumbered by theologies of either pan-Arabism or feelings of patriotism for Egypt or Israel, the Bedouin have discovered superb opportunities for spying and smuggling provided by the warring nations of the Sinai. After World War I, Sinai was described by British Governor Major C.S. Jarvis as "the smugglers' highway." Hashish smuggling from Turkey and Syria to Egypt, across the Sinai, became a major commercial enterprise.

In his book, *Three Deserts,* Jarvis described one instance of Bedouin ingenuity in smuggling hashish. During a police arrest of a clever Bedouin smuggler, it was discovered that the thick hair of the camel had been cut away and packages of hashish neatly glued to the animal's sides. The camel fur was then replaced to hide this valuable stash. Bernstein describes another Bedouin trick of shipping water-tight rubber bags of hashish by boats along the Mediterranean coast, weighing them down with sacks of salt. "If the boats are challenged, the smugglers ditch the bags in the water; the salt dissolves in a few days, causing the bags to rise to the surface, where they can be picked up at a more opportune time. Hashish is familiarly known as 'Sinai Sheikh.' "[15] In 1978, the late Anwar Sadat proclaimed a vision of the Sinai: "Greenery will cover the Peninsula . . . it will become a land of love, peace and coexistence." In some remote regions of the Sinai, at least, part of Sadat's dream is real. Yet, among the Bedouin, poverty is the rule although life in the infinite calm of the desert is free, sociable and far removed from the wars and travails of contemporary life.

Today, Bedouin culture is in retreat. In areas near the Mediterranean coast, the brown-and-white goat-hair tent is giving way to the concrete house. In many places in the Sinai, the tent remains only because Egyptian law prohibits the destruction of a tent-like structure. Inside the tents, copper and brass containers have often been replaced by plastic cups and jugs. In settled villages, Toyota pick up trucks have displaced camels. Young people are no longer taught to water camels and take them to pasture. In the seaside resorts of South Sinai, Bedouin men, wearing Nike running shoes under their *galabiyyahs,* offer camel rides to tourists. Land boundaries that were once controlled by Bedouin customary law courts are now delineated by court order. The picturesque, burnoose-clad tribesman on a camel is often reduced to salaried work. And Bedouin dress and culture are moving into the museums.

The governments of Israel and Egypt are forcing change. In the words of Lila Abu-Lughod, a leading anthropologist of the Bedouin, "For decades the Egyptian authorities have been trying to undermine this form of tribal organization and to get individuals to become tax-paying, school-going, licensed, law abiding, loyal citizens of the state."[16] Pastoral nomads are encouraged, and sometimes forced, to settle on the land, since the authorities know that a settled population is easier to control and to watch. Governments on both sides of the eastern Sinai border are convinced that Bedouin are often double agents as well as expert drug smugglers, which hardens their resolve to tie the Bedouin down.

The transition to farming usually begins with a shift from camels to sheep. Often this change is triggered by the erection of a mosque, the digging of a well, or the building of a government school. Bedouin who are beginning to acquire a taste for settled life will then be drawn into the area. Next, they start small gardens and enroll their sons in the public school, realizing that illiteracy presents major handicaps. Branches of the family will still maintain herds of sheep and goats which they graze on the fringes of the northern desert, but the herders will return at evening to a settlement of government-built, concrete block houses instead of to a desert camp of woolen tents.

Although many desert people fiercely cling to their Bedouin identity, in another generation it is likely that there will be few nomadic Bedouin in the Sinai. The march of modernity challenges the very foundations of Bedouin culture—their ancestral beliefs, their marital roles, their family obligations and their concepts of morality and sexuality. Still, for most Bedouin today, the rules that camels are currency and "life without honor and justice is nothing" still hold true. Free they are born and free they will die.

On the two-hour coastal journey to el-'Arish from the Suez Canal, we drove through dune areas covered with scrub growth. A few hundred yards from the highway, we spied the concrete houses of settled Bedouin nestled behind hillocks. Bedouin women in bright, tribal dresses provided brief splashes of color in a predominantly ochre and gray-green landscape. This route has served for many centuries as the highway of trade from northern Egypt, through el-'Arish and thence to Damascus and Babylon. During centuries past, thousands of camel caravans with guides and guards provided by the Bedouin passed this way. In North Sinai, the lucrative caravan trade has now disappeared into the sands of history. The only sign of commerce along this route was one solitary Bedouin woman selling bright, beaded amulets made in the shape of fish. Some bore verses from the *Qur'an*, others carried written love charms.

El-'Arish today is a modern resort town with a wintertime population of twenty-five thousand people. Beginning in late spring, Egyptians from Cairo flock here to enjoy its sea breezes, almost doubling the number of inhabitants. El-'Arish is the seat of the military Governate of North Sinai. Founded three thousand years ago, it was first used by the Greeks and then by the Romans (the same way that the British used Australia millenia later) as a dumping ground for political enemies and convicted felons. Burton Bernstein reminds us "the town was called Rhinokoloura (city of cut noses) by the Greeks, and later, Rhinocolorum by the Romans."[17] Before banishment of the prisoners to this remote Mediterranean settlement, it was the custom to lop off their noses. Colonel Jarvis wrote in the 1930's that el-'Arish "was populated by all those who had not the guts to go on." Today, el-'Arish is a hodgepodge of Egyptians, Bedouin, Arabs, and other Middle Easterners. An Ottoman fort, dating from the fifteenth century, has almost disappeared and the Egyptian-Israeli Wars have destroyed most vestiges of quaint, colonial architecture. What remains is an undistinguished jumble of concrete houses, military buildings, groves of date palms, hotels, souvenir shops, and pastel-painted condominiums.

Since 1982, over forty Egyptian tourist hotels have mushroomed along the wide, sandy beaches. Samir drove us to a glitzy Sheraton on the western edge of town. This was to be our home for five days. Occupying two rooms, we brought the occupancy rate up by 30 percent. In January, the only visitors to el-'Arish are occasional journalists or foreign-aid delegations who share a concern for the Sinai Bedouin. A group of eleven Germans was staying at the hotel. Some of them represented the German government; others were from a private, charitable group, the Society for the Preservation of Bedouin Culture. The Germans, inveterate travelers to all of the most remote parts of Egypt, have established health clinics and experimental agricultural projects to help the settled Bedouin.

We invited our friend, the lieutenant colonel, to lunch with us before his return to Cairo. In the high-ceilinged splendor of our nearly empty hotel dining room, embellished with metal date palms bearing leaves of glittering gold, we gazed out on the sea. Military salaries are low in Egypt, even for high-ranking officers, and the colonel seemed happy to be treated to a large Egyptian meal. A generous helping of beans made up 50 percent of his lunch order. My meal of two local quail was excellent. Flocks of migratory quail scurry along main highways and small, sandy tracks in North Sinai and are the most abundant form of wildlife. They almost always appear on hotel menus, served up in a variety of culinary ways.

The colonel's parting act was to take us to local military headquarters where we were turned over to a twenty-year-old Egyptian army captain. Were we being demoted? We dropped the colonel off at the local bus station where we watched him hail a cab for his return to Cairo.

I now left the opulent surroundings of the Sheraton and began my exploration of Sinai. With the aid of the Governor General and the North Sinai authorities, who provided military access and guidance to roads not found on standard maps, I poked into innumerable Bedouin villages, and spent the next three days exploring. In North Sinai, the black tents of nomadic tribes are difficult to find, as the vast majority of tribesmen now live in small communities of mud or concrete houses. Each of these houses usually has an open courtyard surrounded by a wall made of brush or mud. In this area, meal preparation and most of life's daily chores take place. Often, in more prosperous settlements, a lemon tree adds a dash of green and yellow to the courtyard. Some settled Bedouin decorate their houses with vivid geometric designs. Occasionally, I saw a white flag erected on a concrete dwelling, a public proclamation called *tabyiid*, or "whitening of the face", which declares that a family member accused of crime has been exonerated of all wrongdoing by his accuser and is now without blame.

It was difficult—and therefore especially gratifying—to find a black tent or group of tents nestled behind hillocks or dunes. The Bedouin women I photographed in front of these tents possessed great dignity and presence. They stood calmly, showing no emotion, not seeming to mind me or my camera.

Southeast of el-'Arish and close to the border of Israel is an oasis of major biblical significance. I had learned about this in an evening I had spent in New York with Tom Pickering, U.S. Ambassador to the United Nations, and Alice, his wife. The Pickerings are deeply attached to Sinai, having camped on many occasions in its remotest areas. With the aid of maps drawn in the seventies during the Egyptian-Israeli conflict and spread out on the table of a New York restaurant, the Pickerings introduced me to historical biblical routes I must follow and to places I must see. The most important of these was a lush oasis, Kadesh Barnea or Moses Valley, located between the Negev and Sinai deserts, eight kilometers southeast of el-Quseima. This oasis is believed to be the site where Moses brought forth water from the rock. Kadesh Barnea is also believed to be the place where the Israelites spent most of their forty years in the wilderness as recounted in the Old Testament. The route we followed led from Wadi el-'Arish to Abu Aweigilla and then on to the Red Sea. The way to the Moses Spring is covered with boulders and the last part of our trip was on foot. We arrived at a sparkling, bubbling outpouring of water, Ein Qudeirat, the largest source of fresh water in the Negev and Sinai peninsula. An hourly discharge of forty to fifty cubic meters suggests that Kadesh Barnea, could easily have supported six hundred Israelite families during their forty-year stay.

At the end of the trip to Kadesh Barnea, we visited Bedouin settlements near the Israeli border where small children proudly produced treasured caches of metal, military helmets and grubby handfuls of empty gun shell casings for my admiration. I was reminded of the grisly tale of an unlucky American journalist who recently, in northern Sinai near the Israeli border, had stepped on a land mine and lost his right arm.

With the help of the Governor General and the Egyptian military in el-'Arish, I was introduced to a tiny band of university teachers and former civil service administrators and other Egyptians who cared passionately about the fate of the Sinai Bedouin and the preservation of their fragile and fleeting culture. They rode with me to villages and spent many hours relating stories of tribal lore.

The images of these excursions into the desert from el-'Arish remain vivid. As the first pale glimmer of morning light creeps over the silent desert, Bedouin men emerge from their low, black tents and gather for communal prayer, prostrating themselves on the sand. Baby sheep and goats wander in and out of the woolen tents. From their perches on the tent roofs, the roosters greet the dawn. Children stir from the ground cloths that serve as beds, and women light small fires of brushwood and prepare glasses of heavily sweetened black tea with which the Bedouin begin each day.

The tents, always pitched facing east, supported by a line of wooden poles made from branches of acacia, ben trees, or wild figs, offer shade from the brutal Sinai sun and provide warmth on frigid winter nights. Waterproofing is assured by the goat hair and sheep wool that expand when wet. Woven cloth dividers separate the men's quarters from that of the women. In the men's section, rugs are spread out to cover the sand. The women occupy one-third of the tent, "the forbidden place," and rarely go into the men's and guest areas. Supplies of grain, dates, and coffee beans are stored in sacks at the back of the tent. Water, the nomad's most precious possession, is stored in tanned and oiled animal water skins called *girbas*. A cubic meter of water is still worth a grain of gold, and the Muzeina of South Sinai still worship a rain goddess, *Umm el-Ghayth*, to whom they offer prayers and oblations.

During my travels south from el-'Arish, I thought of the Bedouin women whose lives, by western standards, are so terribly vulnerable, dependent, lonely, and isolated. In her eloquent contribution to women's studies,[18] anthropologist Lila Abu-Lughod analyzes the symbolic meaning of the oral poetry sung by Awlad 'Ali women of the western desert. These traditional poetic discourses called *ghinnawas* (little songs) are rich expressions of the love, longing, and defiance which these women may not openly utter in a society that believes in polygamy, arranged marriages, and the inferiority of women. The verses, which Professor Abu-Lughod calls "haiku in form but more like American blues in content or emotion," are sung in high-pitched chants or monotones with words often repeated or reversed. In examples of these laments, a woman denies concern about a husband taking another wife but sings of the pain she feels; a young, second wife denies interest in men but sings of a former love; a senior wife accused of sorcery sings of her isolation and loneliness and of being wronged. As songs of protest emanating from the pure simplicity of desert life, the *ghinnawas* are authentic, indigenous expressions of feminism. Formerly sung at weddings, sheep shearings, grain threshings, and tattooings, the *ghinnawas* are now often sung between pauses in cross-stitches during the endless hours that Bedouin women spend embroidering dresses in the tent.

A young Bedouin girl may begin to embroider a dress at the age of nine, carrying the material with her wherever she goes, even out into distant grazing areas. It may take five years to complete the intricate work. The dress will be ready for her to wear at the time of her marriage, usually at age fourteen or fifteen. She will have the embroidery for the rest of her life and, when the black cotton background material wears out, the embroidery will be transferred to another identical black dress. The lovely cross-stitch designs are an important part of the culture and tribal heritage of North Sinai. Many of the cross-stitched patterns closely resemble those of Palestinian Bedouin. This crossing of geographic lines in Bedouin culture is no surprise since such Bedouin traditions of embroidery reach back into history, long before the existence of modern political boundaries.

To preserve the intricately embroidered tribal designs and the Bedouin arts of weaving and embroidery, Mohamed Korayem, former director of development of North Sinai, has established sewing and weaving projects in the villages of North Sinai. According to Mr. Korayem, seventy-two Bedouin families scattered throughout the area are now producing wool rugs using the same patterns and vegetable dyes that have been in place for centuries. To maintain traditional purity, the wool is sometimes dyed in Cairo, as many Bedouin have lost the subtle art of producing vegetable dyes. Mobile sewing projects are now under way to copy and perpetuate the stunning patterns of antique Bedouin embroidery. A museum dedicated to the culture of North Sinai has been established in el-'Arish. Here I saw the finest examples of Sinai Bedouin weaving and embroidery, along with the beautifully crafted iron and copper coffee pots, woven saddle bags, sheepskin waterbags and maroon and green camel bridles. Scholars and students of ethnology believe that in twenty years this may be all that remains of the unique culture of the Sinai Bedouin.

One evening in el-'Arish we were invited to visit a new theater and art center in the city. A troop of Arishi high school students performed a series of Bedouin dances and songs for the benefit of the German delegation. The singer was an authentic Bedouin but the dancers were young Egyptians. It was as if white American high school students were putting on a performance of Harlem break-dancing. At the conclusion of the production, the German guests were asked to parade across the stage while the audience of Egyptian officials and teachers applauded vigorously. Then the dancers motioned our little group of three up onto the stage for a bow, also to the accompaniment of deafening applause.

Every Thursday, the celebrated el-'Arish market is deployed around the city's central mosque. For Bedouin women, market day in el-'Arish is a joyfully anticipated event which breaks the oppressive tedium of the desert. They visit with relatives, exchange gossip about babies and marriages and pick up some much needed cash. On market day, Bedouin women come on foot from long distances, as far away as thirty miles, as far away as Rafah on the Israeli border, Lake Bardawil on the west, and el-Quseima on the south. Unless they own a camel or have access to a pickup truck, they must leave many days earlier, arriving in time to set up their wares in the huge, open section of the market, which by custom, is designated as their special bailiwick. Needing money more than they need their grandmother's worn out *burqu'*, they will sell this veil laden with silver and golden coins to a tourist from Israel or Europe.

In winter, tourists are scarce and the Bedouin may have to part with their elaborately embroidered dresses at a greatly reduced price to members of their own tribe. A Remilaat woman who is busy planting crops and pruning apricot trees may no longer have the long hours of herding time needed to embroider the intricate red-and-green cross-stitching, which is de rigueur in her particular tribe. The dresses of young, unmarried girls are almost always cross-stitched in blue. Upon marriage, these symbols of maidenhood are immediately discarded for reasons of suspected bad luck. They have become a glut on the market.

At the market, I haggled for several orange and rust-colored *burqu'*s. With long chains dangling on the sides decorated with alloyed squares of silver, they jingle cheerfully. Added to the veil are long strings of red, blue and white glass beads, with bits of coral and amber inserted into the strands. The veils are heavily laden with coins from Ceylon and West Africa as well as with contemporary Egyptian piastres. In past centuries, it was said the Bedouin women carried their fortunes on their veils. Most coins that ornament veils today have little value.

The women's market area is only a small part of el-'Arish's Thursday bustle. On some days, a truck will come into town from Cairo, laden with city-made wares. One day, several hundred royal blue sweaters arrived. Within an hour, these cardigans become standard attire for members of the Remilaat tribe. Large numbers of Egyptian merchants in the market sell everything from dish towels to head scarves, or *kaffiyahs*, from cassette tapes to bird cages.

Near the central mosque, Bedouin women hawk hundreds of fluffy, black-and-white rabbits, holding them up by their pink-lined ears to show them off. Nearby, a noisy chicken and bird section is alive with peeps and squawks. Wooden cages crammed full of red-combed roosters and black or browny-red chickens tempt the shopper. In another section, behind the mosque, Bedouin men display fat, white sheep with dark faces and black and brown goats, while they sip tea and brag about their animals.

Grown along the Mediterranean coast, fresh produce is plentiful. Cabbages are gigantic, looking as if they had been injected with some magical hormone. Succulent tomatoes and peppers are lined up, plump, bright red and yellow, like spots of primary colors in a child's painting.

I am still stirred by memories of the brightly hued, hand-embroidered dresses of North Sinai women, of their coin-laden veils hanging heavy over tattooed faces, by the piles of silver jewelry and Maria Theresa coins, Bedouin rugs, and camel blankets—a treasure trove of ethnographic lore, all offered for sale in this fabulous Sinai marketplace.

South to St. Catherine's Monastery

Once more, we headed out into the sea of sand. This time we were going south from the scrub-covered dunes of the el-'Arish littoral into the barren emptiness of Sinai's central interior. Behind us were the dark blue waters of a winter Mediterranean, and the blue and red dories that were part of a small fishing fleet bravely venturing out even on a cold January morning. The empty streets of el-'Arish waited for the annual springtime invasion of Egyptian vacationers. Our destination was Nakhl (the Arabic word for date palm), seventy-five miles south across the desert. Our military escort on this part of the trip was a handsome but taciturn Egyptian captain. We stopped occasionally to photograph the lonely figure of a Bedouin shepherdess or an old woman standing in front of a solitary, black tent. In these remote areas of the Sinai where the Bedouin have almost no contact with the outside world, Egyptian hard candy is a valuable commodity. As soon as the candy appears, Bedouin women frequently run behind a hillock and return with sister shepherds, hands outstretched and faces shyly wreathed in smiles. The Egyptian pound has no meaning here; hard candy is the hard currency of the central Sinai desert. The economic isolation of these people reminds me of the extraordinary barrenness of Sinai, a human vacuum with a population density of fewer than two people per square mile.

At noon we arrived at Nakhl, a dusty little settlement slightly north of dead center Sinai. It was once an important watering place on the pilgrimage to Mecca. An Ottoman fort was erected at Nakhl in the sixteenth century, as protection for pilgrims. Today, Nakhl is merely a small cluster of mud buildings comprised of a medical clinic, a fruit stand, a combination coffee shop and gas station, and the ruined fort. In Nakhl, I saw a camel standing patiently near the gas pumps as if waiting for a refill.

From Nakhl, we drove east and south through el-Thamad on our way to the Gulf of 'Aqaba, crossing flat plains and low mountains. In the afternoon, we arrived at Nuweiba, a seedy resort town on the Sinai coast of the Gulf of 'Aqaba. Only fifteen miles away, across the Gulf, shrouded in mist, lay the mountainous coast of Saudi Arabia. From Nuweiba, a large ferry boat leaves for the 'Aqaba shore several times a day. In Nuweiba, Bedouin are everywhere, many hanging out at the local beachside stands that sell sunglasses and souvenirs. They lead their bedraggled camels down the dusty roads, cadging *baksheesh* and hoping to be photographed. During the Israeli occupation of Sinai, they drank Gold Star Israeli beer with the tourists. Now they beg, something a Bedouin would be ashamed to do. The desert people near Nuweiba are sorry remnants of the noble, proud figures of legend and poetry.

The following day, I was happy to leave tawdry Nuweiba. Less than four hours away south and west was Mt. Sinai and the celebrated St. Catherine's Monastery. We were accompanied by a fifth military escort, an enthusiastic, young Egyptian soldier who spoke some English and had aspirations of becoming a tour guide. He was to remain with us until we returned to Cairo. We discovered later that he was well known to the monks of the Monastery because he had grown up near the village of St. Catherine's.

Through the deep wadis, or valleys, of South Sinai we continued south and west, into the great, coastal mountains. The terrain grew steadily more rugged and soon we were surrounded by jagged, granite cliffs, their vertical sides of red and black volcanic rock shot through with streaks of green. As we approached St. Catherine's village, we began to see a number of small, domed tombs, built of stone and capped by the slender crescent moon of Islam. Devout Bedouin have positioned them on high ground so the tombs can be seen and visited by passing pilgrims. Signs posted near the monuments tell the pilgrim that he is passing the tomb of a great prophet or merely that of a minor holy man. Like scholars who disagree about Shakespeare's identity, Sinai Bedouin may claim five or six different locations for the tombs of their great prophets. To be fair to all believers, a sign is erected at each site, declaring it to be the "true" tomb of the prophet.

We drove through a series of deeply etched valleys cut out of the rock. Suddenly we were stunned to see a standing pond of blue water. In the winter, instant torrential rains and floods can create a temporary lake in a matter of only a few hours. Bedouin take care not to pitch their tents in the deepest part of the long, winding valleys, choosing always a higher site part way up the hill. We passed Bedouin women washing clothes in a temporary basin of rain water and hanging their precious red-and-crimson dresses out to dry on stiff bushes of broom. There was no risk of theft. Under Bedouin tribal law, a bundle hung in a tree can never be touched or disturbed.

We now passed near the huge Plain of Raha, the flatlands where in about 1225 B.C., biblical scholars maintain that the Israelites camped awaiting the Commandments from God. We were soon surrounded by purple, lavender and gold mountains a mile or more high. Southernmost stands Mt. Sinai, also known as Jebel Musa, or Mount Moses, the sacred place where Moses received the Commandments of the Lord. According to the Book of Exodus, Moses and the Israelites were led to Mt. Sinai by a sign of God's presence—a column of smoke or cloud during the day and a column of fire at night.

Each year, tens of thousands of pilgrims and tourists visit the Plain of Raha and the sacred ground is now scarred with motels and restaurants. Arriving at the village of St. Catherine's for lunch, we found that our hotel was an enormous collection of attractively-joined, stone cottages, each with its own fireplace. Many think that these cottages defile the sacred plain and, to be sure, giant wheels, their motifs signifying the martyrdom of St. Catherine, are scattered randomly in open areas between the guest quarters.

At the hotel desk, we met the renowned Dr. John Swanson, director of Field Studies for the American University in Cairo, a distinguished scholar and a walking encyclopedia on everything Egyptian. Dr. Swanson was to accompany us throughout South Sinai and return with us to Cairo. The moment he began to speak about St. Catherine's, we realized our good fortune in having him as our friend and mentor for four days.

After lunch, we hiked a mile up the high valley where St. Catherine's Monastery is situated. The winter air was crisp and invigorating. On this January day, there was no snow though it often falls in these high regions. Approaching the dramatic, granite walls surrounding the Monastery, some decorated with Maltese crosses, we climbed a large rock to reach a better vantage point. Still breathless, we got our first full view of the Monastery, a proud symbol of sixteen hundred years of Christian monasticism in the heart of Muslim territory. Built in the sixth century A.D., the Monastery has never been burned, captured or destroyed. It was late afternoon and the western sun shone on the towering, dark green cypress trees behind the holy fortress. Beginning in the sixth century, Byzantine monks carved 3700 steps in the steep rock to the 7497-foot high summit of Mt. Sinai, but today the arduous, three-hour climb is undertaken mainly by hardy backpackers who spend the night on the mountaintop in order to see the dawn from this most sacred of places.

For the local Jebeliya Bedouin, too, Mt. Sinai, is a holy site. On the top of the mountain stands a Greek Orthodox chapel as well as a small mosque. The mosque's doorway was once blackened and stained with the blood of sheep and goats sacrificed by the local Jebeliya. These Bedouin honor Moses and believe him to be the source of rain. Every summer, the major Bedouin tribes of South Sinai—the Muzeina, the Awlad Sa'id, and the Jebeliya—meet near here for the feast of Nabi Saleh, who is the most important prophet for the South Sinai Bedouin. Traditionally the repast has consisted of a roasted camel stuffed with a roasted sheep—stuffed in turn with a roasted goat. The Bedouin eat the slaughtered animals, socialize, and reaffirm their intertribal ties. Although much less elaborate today, this feast is still the most important ritual for the South Sinai Bedouin and the only occasion when large numbers of different tribes come together.

The village of St. Catherine's, a half mile away from the Monastery, houses a bakery, souvenir shops, a gas station and mud brick houses belonging to the Jebeliya. Twenty miles west of St. Catherine's village is Wadi Feiran (the Valley of Mice), the most fertile area of the Sinai peninsula. Nestled between towering, granite mountains, this oasis lies at the foot of Jebel Serbal, another mountain sometimes said to be the true site of the Ten Commandments. Called "the Pearl of the Sinai," Wadi Feiran is filled with sharp-thorned acacias, groves of date palms, and thousands of tamarisk trees which are believed to have supplied the Israelites with the manna of the Old Testament. A population of settled tribesmen, affluent by Bedouin standards, live here producing maize, wheat, and fruit.

Since the fourth century A.D., the hills and mountains around Mt. Sinai have been honeycombed with caves of holy, Christian hermits who settled here to be close to the sacred place where God first spoke to man. In the fourth century, monks living near the Chapel at the "burning bush" were repeatedly attacked by Bedouin and Nubian raiders. According to Monastery legend, many holy men were murdered as the settlement was plundered by nomads who ate the holy wafers that symbolized the body of Christ.

The most sacred part of St. Catherine's Monastery is the Chapel, marking the place where the Burning Bush, from which God spoke to Moses, is believed to have stood. Outside the Chapel is a living bush, still believed to have been propagated from the original.

In the sixth century, a delegation of Sinai monks traveled to Constantinople and successfully persuaded the Emperor Justinian to protect the holy site by founding a fortress-monastery in the wadi, or valley, at the foot of Mt. Sinai. Burton Bernstein describes the complications: one Doulas was engaged to construct the fortress from five-hundred-and-thirty-five-foot-square blocks of granite. The builder located the fortress at the foot of Mt. Sinai, a strategically unsound position. For this unfortunate decision, Doulas was summarily executed by Justinian once the Emperor learned that to lay siege to the Monastery, all the then hostile Bedouin had to do was to roll stones down the mountain into the fortress structure.

Today, Mt. Sinai remains a focus of faith for the world's three major monotheisms: Islam, Judaism and Christianity. The chancel of the Church of the Transfiguration houses the bones of St. Catherine who, according to legend, was martyred in the fourth century, her body broken by being strapped to a wheel. The story goes that angels flew her bones to the top of Mt. St. Catherine, a nearby peak that is even higher than Mt. Sinai, and from there, the remains were taken to the Monastery. Here they remain, resting in an elaborate reliquary inside the basilica. The legend is that St. Catherine's bones exuded a holy oil that possessed miraculous healing powers. Pilgrims traveled great distances to obtain a tiny vial of the holy elixir.

As a Christian monastery, St. Catherine's came to face grave dangers from Islamic conquerors who occupied Sinai in the seventh century. According to tradition, the monks at the Monastery requested protection of the Prophet Muhammed, and today the monks of St. Catherine's proudly exhibit a letter signed with the handprint of Muhammed (he could not write) guaranteeing the protection of the Monastery. The monks believe that without this covenant of immunity, the Monastery would have been sacked and plundered long ago. Muhammed's guarantee was not always effective. In the early eleventh century A.D., Sultan al-Hakim dispatched troops from Cairo to demolish the Monastery. It is reported that the local monks adroitly saved the day by quickly erecting a mosque within the Monastery walls. The mosque continues to be used today by members of the local Jebeliya Bedouin tribe.

A thousand years ago, there were three or four hundred monks in residence at St. Catherine's, but now there are fewer than twenty, mostly from Greece and Cyprus. For most of its fourteen hundred years, the Monastery has sat peacefully in Islamic territory, welcoming Muslim as well as Christian travelers, guarded by a hereditary tribe of Bedouin and, in medieval times, even subsidized by a succession of caliphs.

Aside from its sacred location, St. Catherine's is world famous for its icons and its library. It possesses the only twenty-seven icons predating the iconoclastic movement of the eighth and ninth centuries. In the narthex of the church is an icon of the Virgin Mary that experts believe may be the oldest in the world. Second only in importance to that of the Vatican, the manuscript library holds a priceless collection of ancient Greek, Syriac, and Arabic manuscripts, "most of it not properly arranged," as one

Western guide book tartly notes. Yet, since World War II more than two thousand documents have been microfilmed. The library also houses a part of the celebrated Codex Sinaiticus, one of the world's oldest surviving Bibles, dating to the fourth century. Other parts of this biblical treasure were "removed" in 1859 by the German scholar K. Von Tischendorf, acting on behalf of the Tsar of Russia. This most precious manuscript was then purchased in 1933 by the British Museum where it is kept to this day.

Since the sixth century, one of the most important wishes of the monks of St. Catherine's has been that the sacred Monastery be their last resting place. But the cemetery at the Monastery is tiny. Deceased monks are buried there, but to make room for successors the bones are exhumed after five years and heaped in a large open bin in the ossuary.

St. Stephanos, who died in 580 A.D., sits today in a large glassed-in box in the charnel house, a macabre figure dressed in purple and blue robes and cowl, with bits of dried flesh clinging to his bones. In life, St. Stephanos sat half way up the 3700 steps which led to the summit of Mt. Sinai. There, he delivered arbitrary judgments on the spiritual purity of pilgrims who were clambering toward the summit. If St. Stephanos decided that they were impure or undeserving, he sent them back down to the valley.

For over three thousand years, from Justinian to Golda Meir, all nations that controlled the Sinai took St. Catherine's Monastery under their protection. And Mt. Sinai was protected, too, by an apocryphal injunction: "Whoever toucheth the mount shall surely be put to death, saith the Lord." The principal threats to this holiest place now seem to come from promoters of tourism. Egypt needs hard currency. Tour buses are bringing hordes to the holy places in the valley. Thirty thousand visitors now come each year to Mt. Sinai. There has been nightmarish talk of constructing a cable car up the side of the Holy Mountain, striking fear in the heart of St. Catherine's small band of monks. But Father Good Angel, who came to the Monastery in 1927, takes a calmer view. "Only God knows if it will happen."

This Bedouin belongs to the Sawarka tribe which is found between Rafa and Sheikh Zuwaid in North Sinai. The style ▷ of the *burqu'*, or face mask, worn after marriage, varies from tribe to tribe. If a woman is wealthy, half of the coins will be of real gold, while the rest will be gilded. Cowrie shells ornament her headband.

Overleaf: The winter sun sets over a timeless, bucolic scene in the North Sinai. Since early morning, women and ▷▷ children have tended the flocks of goats and sheep which graze contentedly on an abundance of winter greenery. The women will mount their camels and the children will scurry after them, making sure no straggling sheep is forgotten.

Second Overleaf: Boats from a small fishing fleet on the beach at el-'Arish. With the forests long gone from Sinai, these ▷▷▷ craft must be built with timber from Europe. In the folk tradition of Mediterranean fishermen, stern paintings usually depict fish and sea monsters.
Until modern times, the Sinai Bedouin would not touch fish, saying to the coastal dwellers of el-'Arish: "You are eating the snake of the sea." Now many of these desert people are fishing or engaged in jobs connected with the industry.

Scrub-covered dunes line the road between the Suez Canal and el-'Arish. A North Sinai Bedouin stands near the roadway, watching the infrequent traffic.

In North Sinai, at the el-'Arish Thursday market, a treasure trove of ethnographic lore is offered for sale ▷ by Bedouin women whose coin-laden veils hang heavy over their tattooed faces. They sell piles of silver jewelry, Maria Theresa coins, Bedouin rugs, and hand-embroidered dresses. The eye painted on the wall wards off evil spirits.

◁◁ *Previous page:* At sunset in North Sinai, a member of the Sawarka tribe leads her extra camel home across the desert. Both camels are laden with castor leaves which will be used for camel fodder.

This woman of the Remilaat tribe wears a *shanaf* (nose ring), a still popular ornament among the Bedouin of North Sinai.

◁ The Thursday market at el-'Arish in North Sinai is a moving kaleidescope of vegetables, fruit, sheep, rabbits and goats.

◁◁ *Previous page:* A Bedouin customary law court is held in the reception room of the 'Arrada tribe in the village of Kharruba, near Sheikh Zuwaid. Shaykh Salaama ibn 'Arrada is presiding. No Bedouin tribunal ever begins its deliberations without the rituals of coffee preparation (strictly a male prerogative). Before the court session starts, the judge's assistants prepare pots for making various Arabic blends. Coffee pouring always begins on the right.

The preparation ritual is as important as the coffee itself. Water is boiled in a blackened copper pot. Coffee beans are roasted to a light brown in a shallow skillet and then beaten by the "sultan of the coffee" with a large wooden pestle until the beans have been crushed into a powder. Coffee is served in small cups without handles. Aromatic cardamom, a favorite spice in Sinai, enhances the flavor and is often added.

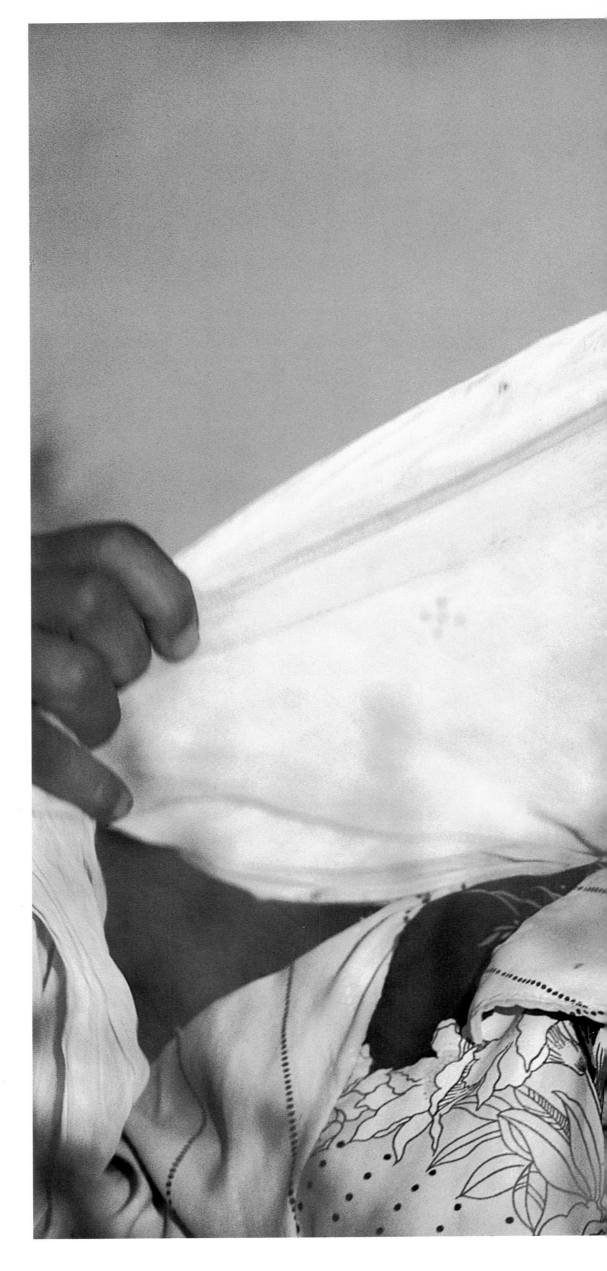

At el-Herosh, a tiny settlement in North Sinai, a modest Bedouin woman momentarily uncovers her face which is usually concealed from the eyes of strangers by a white headcloth.

Overleaf: In South Sinai, winter rain showers may occur suddenly. These Bedouin women take advantage of a rare, temporary pool of rainwater to wash their clothes and hang them to dry on broom bushes. According to Bedouin tribal law, anything hung in trees or on bushes is inviolable.

This tattooed Bedouin woman wears an elaborately embroidered dress which, by its special stitchery, denotes membership in the Sawarka tribe. In the past, girls were usually tattooed at five or six years of age. Their skin was pricked in patterns such as bird or flower designs, some quite intricate and all considered beautiful. Indigo was rubbed into the puncture marks. Indelible blue marks remained on the front of the chin, the back of the right hand, the foot, the forehead, or the middle of the bosom. Tattooing seems to be going out of fashion for young Bedouin girls. It is rarely seen in Sinai in anyone under eighteen.

This woman of North Sinai is a member of the Remilaat tribe. Bedouin women who are past the age ▷ of childbearing become more relaxed in their daily relationships with men. They leave their faces uncovered, talk freely with men of any age, argue frequently and are not afraid to speak out publicly. On occasion, they may even enter the male part of the tent. In many camps, a head woman, usually the wife of the sheikh of the camp, greets guests if males are absent.

◁◁ *Previous page:* A pastoral scene in North Sinai reflects images of the Old Testament.

A Bedouin shepherdess in North Sinai.

These girls of the Bedouin Jebeliya tribe live in the village of St. Catherine's, a few kilometers from the Monastery. The Egyptian government runs a free school here. Eighty percent of the boys attend, but far fewer girls. Teachers come from towns in the Nile Valley and the curriculum bears scant cultural connection to anything relating to Bedouin life in the bleak mountains of Sinai.

◁ In Sinai, white flags are planted near homes when their owners have safely returned from the pilgrimage to Mecca. The flags may also signify that peace has been established between warring families and that accusations of wrongdoing have been withdrawn by the accuser.

Overleaf: The twisted road from Nuweiba (on Sinai's Gulf of 'Aqaba coast) to St. Catherine's Monastery goes ▷▷ through deep valleys and mountain passes. Along the way, there are scattered camps of nomadic Bedouin. Camel saddles become convenient seats or backrests as families gather around the cooking fires near their fringed, goat-hair tents.

It is likely that this middle-aged Bedouin is less fastidious in his standards of religious devotion than the urban ▷
or village Muslim. Yet, when the rooster crows each morning, male members of the Bedouin camps still gather
outside their tents and engage in the first of the five daily communal prayers, prostrating themselves in the desert
sand as they face Mecca.

Overleaf: On the road from the east to St. Catherine's, the tomb of a minor holy man is crowned by a crescent ▷▷
moon.

This Bedouin youth is wearing a *kaffiyah*, a headdress in the Jordanian fashion. The ▷
zippered pullover suggests that he has shopped in el-Tor, the capital of South Sinai.
But the chance that he can read or write is less than one in ten.

◁◁ *Previous page:* Gas stations are infrequently found in Sinai; camels are still the most
efficient and inexpensive mode of transportation for traversing long stretches of
desert wasteland.

In the winter months when sporadic rains water the desert, dotting it with scattered clumps of green scrub, the camel survives for weeks by eating plants.

In the Bedouin camp of the Muzeina tribe, the wedding day arrives and a *birza*, or special wedding tent is set up. The South Sinai bride is led to the *birza* on a decorated camel provided by the groom. She circles the tent three times, then dismounts and enters the tent with a female attendant. Here she remains while the groom feasts with his friends in the men's tent.

◁ The house or tent of a Bedouin is always surrounded by an invisible boundary mark, its privacy inviolable to strangers. The bounds are determined by "a stick's throw." Under Bedouin law, the penalty for a violation may be the transfer of a goat, sheep or camel to the injured party. These Muzeina sheepherding women in South Sinai are wearing their every-day clothes.

◁◁ *Previous two openings:* Each of the brown, goat-hair tents of this Muzeina Bedouin camp in South Sinai has a cloth divider that separates the men's and women's quarters. The women are in charge of weaving, repairing and stowing the tents when camp is struck. The Bedouin abhor waste and trash, and leave almost no traces when they move.

Sometime after the first century A.D., the wheeled cart disappeared as the principal means of heavy transport in Egypt. It was replaced by the camel, surely God's clumsiest and most ungainly creature. But in Bedouin poetry this awkward beast is "the ship of the desert." She can be ridden, loaded with heavy baggage, harnessed to a plow, and used to traverse difficult terrain. Moreover, she can be milked, eaten, or traded for goods or wives.

◁ At age eighty, Abdul Mutullib is the oldest man in a Bedouin Muzeina camp of black, goat-hair tents located in South Sinai between St. Catherine's Monastery and Wadi Feiran.

Overleaf: Near St. Catherine's village in South Sinai, this elderly Bedouin of the Jebeliya tribe guards the memorial of the Prophet ▷▷
Nabi Saleh. Pilgrims who enter this tomb-like structure stop to pray and cover themselves with dust from its interior.

No one knows the true identity of Nabi Saleh. Some say he was one of the long line of prophets preceding Muhammed. Others hold that he was the progenitor of the Bani Saleh tribe. Some Bedouin believe that Nabi Saleh had mystical powers and produced a she camel from a rock at the top of Mt. Sinai.

Ahmet, a member of the Jebeliya Bedouin tribe, stands by the door- ▷
way to the ossuary of St. Catherine's Monastery. Ahmet has loyally
served the monks here for over fifty years. The Jebeliya (the name
means "people of the mountains") are a tribe of the South Sinai
descended from Balkan slaves sent in the sixth century by Byzantine
emperor, Justinian, to serve the monks at St. Catherine's. Because of
their foreign blood, the Jebeliya are scorned by other Bedouin tribes,
and intermarriage with them is virtually forbidden by custom.

◁◁ *Previous page:* A view from the north of St. Catherine's Monastery in
the mountains of South Sinai. The heart of the Monastery is the
Church of the Transfiguration. Its blue-tiled roof appears next to the
bell tower and the white-domed mosque. The latter was built in the
twelfth century at the behest of a sultan of Egypt who, in return,
guaranteed the inviolability of the Monastery. The bells in the tower
awaken the monks every morning with thirty-three strokes, signifying
the years of Christ's life.

At St. Catherine's Monastery in South Sinai, roofed passageways give access to small courts and staircases of bewildering complexity. Today, only fifteen Greek Orthodox monks still live here. Father Makarios, an American monk from Salt Lake City, stands in an inner courtyard.

Veiled Bedouin, a member of the Jebeliya tribe, in St. Catherine's village, South Sinai.

In Sinai, plant life bravely takes hold wherever it can ▷
find a drop of rainwater. Finally smothered by sand,
the bleached remains of a broom bush stand forlornly
on a steep slope. In the background is a rock formation of so-called Nubian sandstone.

Overleaf: Late afternoon light in Aswan has a special ▷▷
luminous quality. Here, *feluccas* glide along the river
with their swallow-tailed sails mirrored in the tran-
quil waters of the Nile. Above, with a commanding
view of Aswan, stands the tomb of the Aga Khan
(1887–1957), the *imam,* or spiritual leader, of the
Nizari branch of Ismailis. The Begum, his widow,
ordered a fresh red rose to be placed daily on his
white, marble sarcophagus.

The Nile Valley

The Nile Valley

The Path of the Nile

Since the New Stone Age, the world's longest river has ruled the people who lived along its banks. Herodotus, the fifth century Greek historian, wrote "Egypt is the Nile and the Nile is Egypt." Without the Nile, there could be no Karnak, no Sphinx, no Abu Simbel. From the days of the First Dynasty of the Pharaohs, the ancient Egyptians assiduously studied the habits of the river. Obliged to govern a land without rain, the ministers of the Pharaoh anxiously measured its level and regularly scrutinized its flow. The early Egyptians worshipped the Nile God, Hopi, and his wife, Rebati, and annually celebrated the eleventh day of June when the river began to rise. This was the "Night of the Tear," when the Goddess Isis wept for her slain husband, Osiris. Later, in August, Egyptians honored the Misra, when the river reached its peak and then subsided, leaving an abundance of fertile silt behind. But the prayers for floodwaters and for the rich soil they carried from Ethiopia often went unanswered. In her book, *Nile Reflections,* Doreen Anwar reports a 5000-year-old inscription written by the Pharaoh Zoser on a rock south of Aswan at the First Cataract of the Nile:

> This is to inform you of the sorrow which has afflicted me upon my great throne . . . for the Nile has not risen for seven years . . . There is no food of any kind . . . and when the granaries are opened, nothing but air issues from them.[1]

While the patterns of the annual flood have been known since earliest times, the ancient Egyptians did not know where their great river was born. In the fifth century B.C., Herodotus wrote "the sources of the Nile no one can give any account . . . it enters Egypt from parts beyond."[2] Thanks to the intrepid German explorer, Burkhart Waldecker, who discovered its source in 1937, we now know that the life of the Nile begins in a tiny stream of spring water issuing from a hillside deep in south central Africa, in what is now the nation of Burundi. This small ribbon of water begins near the snow-capped Mountains of the Moon discovered by the indefatigable explorer, Henry Morton Stanley, in 1888, only one day after his Mahdi bearers had deserted him. Through dense, tropical jungle, the stream now heads north across Rwanda and Tanzania to Lake Victoria, a great, fresh water, inland sea that is about the size of Ireland. Lake Victoria was created nearly a million years ago when a gradual warping of the earth west of the lake at the Rift Valley in Kenya caused the blockage of four rivers. Formerly one of the world's great ecological treasures, the lake today is slowly dying due to the introduction of the monstrous, cannibal, Nile perch, a six-foot "elephant of the water," often the size of a man. The perch has practically cleared the lake of 400 rare species of fish. Lake Victoria's fisheries appear to be doomed.

Still only 350 miles from its source, the Nile emerges at Jinja on the northern shore of Lake Victoria. Renamed at this point the Victoria Nile, the river roars over the Ripon Falls and plunges into the steamy valley below, a tropical paradise of egrets, spoonbills, and crocodiles. Near here, at Entebbe, a band of Israeli commandos, in a great triumph over international terrorism on July 2, 1976, plucked 104 hostages from under the nose of the African dictator, Idi Amin.

The boiling, and as yet unnavigable, river now works its way northward, over a chain of rapids. Fifty miles later, it suddenly becomes calm. Small steamers and boats come into view. Just north of the Equator, the Nile widens to a thousand yards. The Victoria Nile enters the muddy waters of Lake Kioga, where it flows through sixty sleepy miles of water lilies and hyacinths. Leaving the lake on the northern shore, the river suddenly turns west, hits a rocky bottom and once more grows narrow, swift and deep. Suddenly the river drops 150 feet over the thundering Murchison Falls whose bathing pools were once the ancient home of thousands of crocodiles, rhinos, elephants and hippopotamuses. The Nile then skirts the northern tip of Lake Albert, a powerful feeder lake which doubles the volume of the river's water. At the turn of the century, the only map of this area was French. It provided no detail except "Les éléphants y sont trés nombreux." As the mighty stream pushes north to the southern border of the Sudan, it acquires its second name, the Albert Nile, a 150-mile navigable stretch.

At the Sudan border, the river is rechristened the White Nile, also known locally as the Bahr el Jebel ("Sea of the Mountains"). Deep in the steamy swamplands of the southern Sudan, the river now passes by the stilt-supported papyrus huts of the Dinka, the dominant tribe of the southern Sudan. The Dinka worship their cattle, which are ranked considerably above humans in value and spiritual importance. Seven-foot tall Dinka tribesmen are employed as doormen in hotels in Khartoum.

Traveling through giant reeds and papyrus grasses often eighteen feet high, the river soon enters the dreaded and disease-infested Sudd, Arabic for "obstacle," the world's largest swamp. In this monstrous mass of water courses choked with hyacinths and great matted islands of floating reeds, the Nile loses 40 percent of its volume to evaporation. In this almost inpenetrable morass, scores of explorers have perished and, in some places, even the rhinoceros has difficulty moving. The Sudd occupies 40,000 square miles, an area about the size of Ohio.

Aided by a rainfall of upwards of five inches a day during the monsoon season, the Nile pushes on through the tangled swamp. In the northern part of the Sudd, at Adak, the river passes through an area of contemporary human tragedy. It enters the huge Equitoria province of the eternally troubled country of Sudan.

After gently making its sinuous way through the bamboos, papyrus, elephant grass and dense forests of the central Sudan, the Nile arrives at Kosti, a bird-watcher's paradise, the winter home of millions of screaming ibis, cranes and other waders migrating from the north. One hundred fifty miles later, the river finally reaches the once enchanted but now war-torn Sudanese capital of Khartoum. The capital city is a parched hotbox of taxis and camels which still poke along the streets laid out by Lord Kitchener in the design of a Union Jack. In Khartoum, the White Nile is joined by the Blue Nile. In its journey to the deserts of Sudan, the Blue Nile has come two thousand miles from the 6000-foot-high Lake Tana in northern Ethiopia. As it joins the White Nile, the Blue Nile is a virtual tidal wave in the spring months and at this time of year, it is believed to contribute 80 percent of the volume of both streams. In January, the Blue Nile subsides and yields to that steady stream, the White Nile. As the united river leaves Khartoum, it is a brown, sleepy stream that still has two thousand miles to go on its way to the Nile Delta and then to the Mediterranean.

Two hundred miles downstream from Khartoum at Meroe, there are two hundred pyramids in the desert. Soon, more temples and fortresses are in sight. The Nile twists and turns, reversing its direction for several hundred miles before regaining its heading to the north. Just above the Fourth Cataract at Napata, the river enters the ancient home of the Kushites who, in the eighth century B.C., breezed down the Nile, conquered Egypt, and established an empire reaching as far south as Khartoum. The Pharaoh Tutankhamun so despised the black people from Kush that he had their images embroidered on the soles of

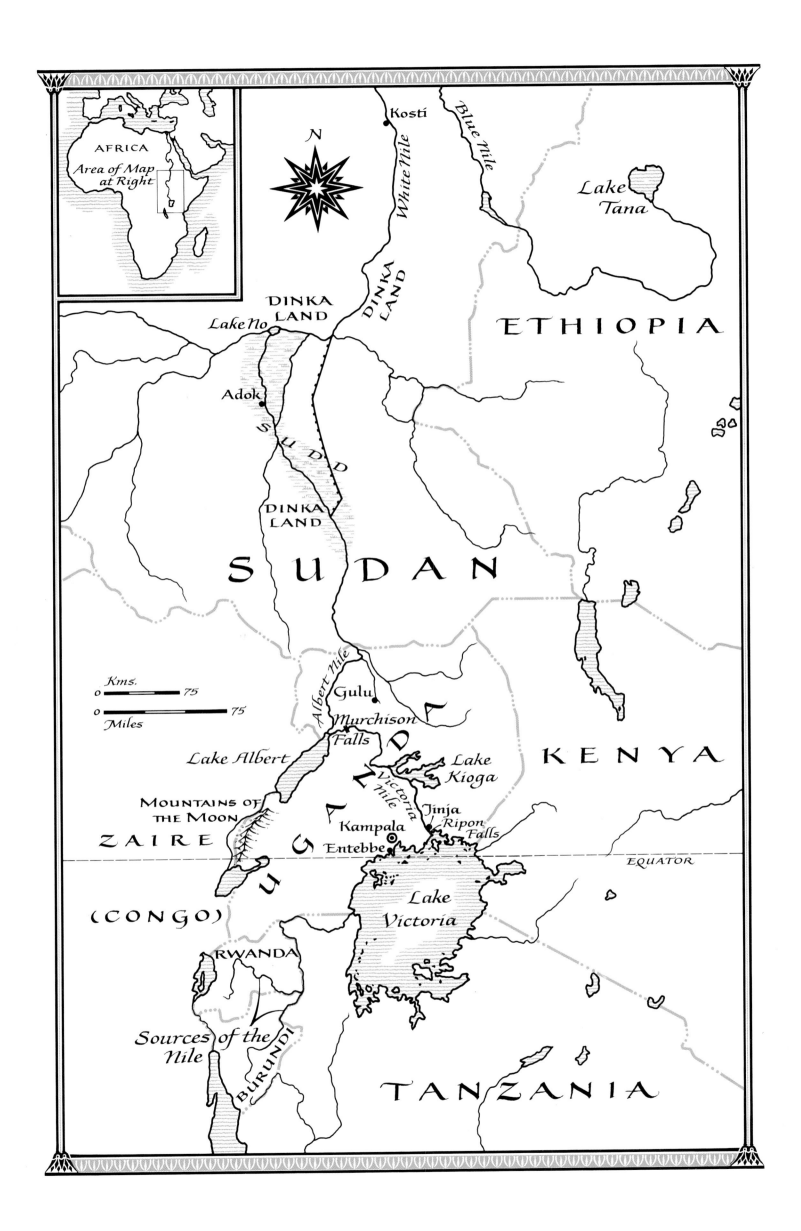

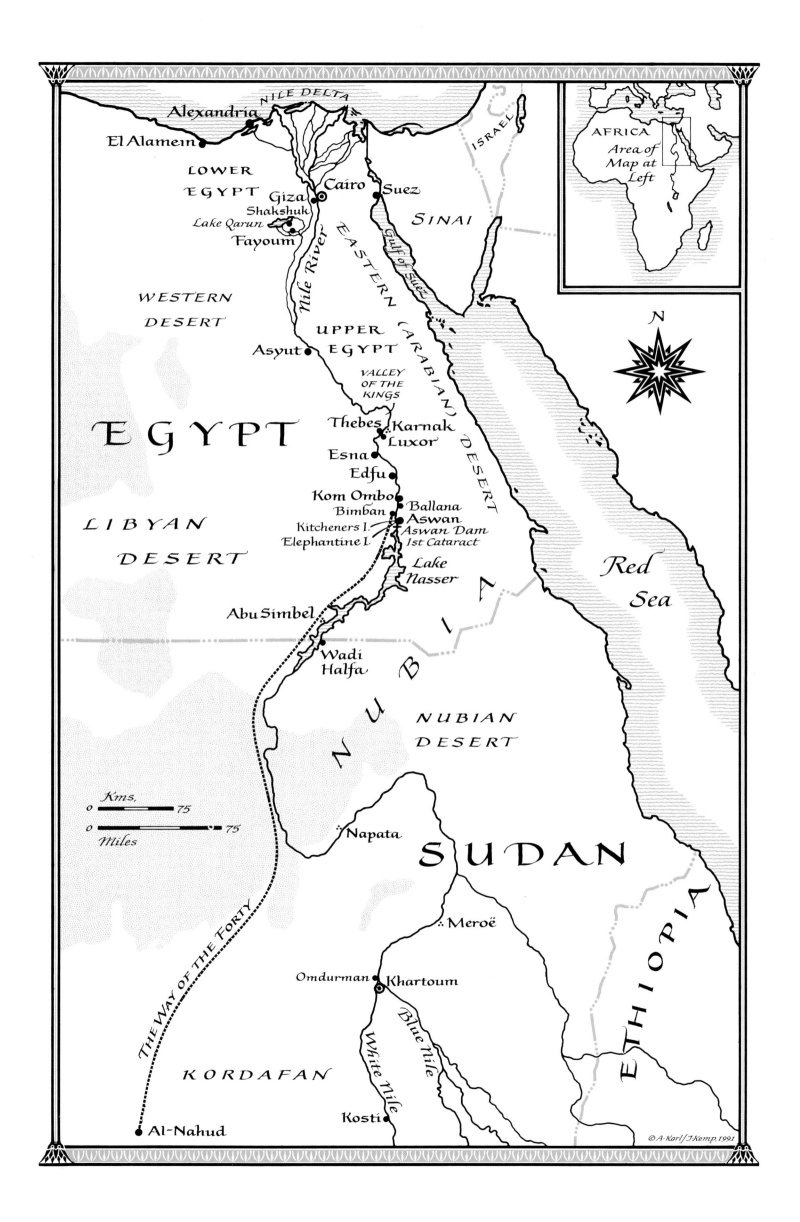

AFRICA
Area of Map at Left

NILE DELTA

Alexandria

El Alamein

LOWER
EGYPT

Cairo

Giza

Shakshuk

Lake Qarun

Fayoum

Suez

SINAI

Gulf of Suez

ISRAEL

WESTERN
DESERT

Nile River

UPPER
EGYPT

Asyut

VALLEY OF THE KINGS

EGYPT

Thebes

Karnak

Luxor

Esna

Edfu

Kom Ombo

Bimban

Ballana

Kitcheners I.

Aswan

Elephantine I.

Aswan Dam

1st Cataract

EASTERN (ARABIAN) DESERT

LIBYAN
DESERT

Lake Nasser

Red Sea

Abu Simbel

N U B I A

Wadi
Halfa

Kms.
0   75

Miles
0   75

NUBIAN
DESERT

Napata

SUDAN

Meroë

THE WAY OF THE FORTY

Omdurman

Khartoum

Blue Nile

White Nile

KORDAFAN

ETHIOPIA

Kosti

Al-Nahud

© A. Karl / J. Kemp, 1991

his sandals. The Nile north of Khartoum is famous, too, as the site of titanic struggles between the most successful of the Mahdis, Muhammed Ahmad, and Charles George "Chinese" Gordon in the 1880s. Possibly abetted by a competing Mahdi from the eastern Sudan, who was reported to be able to fly around in his bed, the Mahdists had the effrontery to march into Khartoum carrying the head of a British colonel on a Dervish spear. Lord Kitchener then summarily crushed the infidels at Omdurman near Khartoum.

As the river continues to snake its way north from Khartoum, the tropics have been left behind and the hippopotamus has become rare. The Nubian desert now borders the Nile as it enters the northern Sudan. This is the homeland of the proud Nubians who once provided soldiers for the pharaoh's armies but later came to rule Egypt three thousand years ago. After the birth of Christ, Egyptians, Persians, Greeks and Romans came to Nubia to find such treasures as cattle, slaves, gold and ivory. It was near the river in Nubia, just north of the present Egyptian-Sudanese frontier at Abu Simbel, that a Swiss traveler in 1813 stumbled upon the huge, carved heads of Ramses the Great, barely visible in the desert sand.

For the next two hundred miles north of Abu Simbel, the Nile becomes the two thousand-square-mile Lake Nasser, whose stored-up water irrigates about six million acres of Egyptian farmland to the north. Still, the Nile valley is able to produce only about half the crops that fifty-five million Egyptians consume every year. At the top of Lake Nasser is the sleepy town of Aswan, once a southerly anchor of the Roman Empire. In his effort to find the source of the Nile, Herodotus reached the First Cataract at Aswan in 460 B.C. before turning back. Known as the Nice of the Nile, Aswan has the finest winter climate on earth. At this winter watering hole for wealthy Egyptians, the Nile turns blue in the evening against a background of purple mountains, gray-green palms and thorny acacias. The combined Egyptian and African flavor of the town is broadcast by shops full of elephant feet, python skins, and Sudanese baskets, by the Nubian villages on Elephantine Island, by the scores of *feluccas* gently working the river, and by the eternal vision of Egypt's most traditional source of irrigation—the *saqiyeh*, or familiar waterwheel, turned by blindfolded oxen. Leaving Aswan, the Nile once more becomes a slender ribbon of water bordered by the Libyan Desert on the west and the Eastern Desert to the east. Four hundred and fifty miles south of Cairo and just above Nasser City, are the resettlement villages of Ballana and Kom Ombo, the new homes of the sixty thousand Nubians who were displaced by the Aswan High Dam. A quarter of a century after they were uprooted from their homes at the bottom of Lake Nasser, they have become successful farmers living in colorfully painted houses on well-kept dirt. However, many Nubians still talk of going home. After they were dispossessed, many Nubians sadly moved north carrying sacks of Nubian earth. In Nubia's Kom Ombo is the site of a fine Ptolemaic temple. The temple houses dusty stacks of sacred, mummified crocodiles whose stiff corpses are sources of macabre fascination for river travelers.

North of Aswan at Bimban, the Nile traveler is likely to see large caravans of camels that are on the last leg of their scorching, nine hundred-mile trek from al-Nahud in the camel-breeding grasslands of Kordofan Province in central Sudan. This ancient route is known as the *Darb al-Arbain*, or "The Way of Forty," being the approximate number of days it requires the Sudanese camel drovers to complete the trip to the famous Imbaba market in a Cairo suburb. The trail bosses navigate this prehistoric desert route at night by keeping the North Star on their left cheek.

Louis Werner provides a splendid account of the snorting, pawing and slurping of the camels at the fifteen-minute rest stop at Bimban for the evening prayer. After urinating in unison, the camels simply stare at their own reflections in the Nile.[3] It has been said that at first sight, the decorated camel, stretching its long neck, looks like a skinny, old Englishwoman sitting bejewelled in her box at the opera.

North of Aswan, contemporary village life along the Nile comes into full view. Old women wearing black headcloths stand in doorways, men ride donkeys, bullocks plow fields, and yoked oxen turn the old wooden wheels. The peasants still use a primitive wooden hoe to loosen the soil around the finest cotton in the world. Here and there along the Nile, women squat and do laundry at the muddy river bank, old men wash in the river in preparation for prayers, and peasants unload bundled stacks of pale-green sugar cane from the backs of camels. Mud-brick houses are decorated with painted camels and the words of the Prophet.

The Upper Nile continues to be a stage set for goats, barking dogs, handsome Egyptian donkeys, and dreaded scorpions. The Nile and its embankment are still bedecked with feathery reeds, yellow-flowered cacti, blue lotus plants and white water lilies. But Nile crocodiles are long since gone, thriving now only in Lake Nasser. Even the graceful and versatile papyrus, once picked by the Egyptian slaves and used to produce mats, rope and sandals and to send rolled, written messages to Damascus and Athens, is now less evident along the banks of the river. No matter how small, each village has its own mosque and minaret.

On the river, north to Edfu, sixty miles above Aswan, the Nile is bordered by the Libyan Desert on the west and the Arabian Desert on the east. The river now passes the town of Edfu, home of a perfectly-preserved Ptolemaic temple, completed in the second century B.C., a thousand years after Karnak and Abu Simbel. The last reach of the Nile ends at Luxor, four thousand miles from its beginnings in Burundi. Here, thirty-five centuries ago, god-like pharaohs presided over the glory of the Egyptian Theban Empire. Here was the center of all wealth and power in the Mediterranean and Middle East. In this most majestic city of the ancient world, the traveler finds today a prodigious collection of temples, statues, obelisks and tombs. Centuries after the flowering of the glorious Theban Kingdom, Homer described its wealth and glory:

> Egyptian Thebes where the houses overflow with the greatest troves
>   of treasure.
> Thebes with the hundred gates and through each gate battalions,
> two hundred fighters surge to war with teams and chariots[4]

Luxor achieved the heights of its influence in the Seventeenth Dynasty around 1650 B.C. Its power continued until the Twentieth Dynasty, about 1085 B.C. Finally, the pharaohs disappeared from their beloved river. A Nubian king entered Thebes in 750 B.C. and became master of all Egypt. Two thousand years later, on November 26, 1922, English Egyptologist Howard Carter made a small opening in a doorway that blocked the entrance to a tomb hidden in the secluded valley among the golden hills known as the Valley of the Kings. By flickering candlelight, he was able to make out "everywhere the glint of gold." Here, amassed before him, were treasures far more fabulous than all of Ali Baba's riches. Piled helter skelter were golden beds made to represent gracefully elongated lions' bodies, a dazzling golden throne ornamented with lions' heads, glistening gold sarcophagi, and, most important of all, the shining death mask of the boy king, Tutankamun, represented as the God of the Sun.

Life in the Villages

North, on the route to Cairo from the First Cataract of the Nile at Aswan is a narrow five-hundred-fifty-mile-long valley of remarkably fertile land enclosed on either side by the rocky cliffs of the desert. Thanks to the work of the Blue Nile in carrying its bounty of soil from the highlands of Ethiopia, the Nile Valley supports ten million Egyptians in Upper Egypt, some in good-sized towns, but most in large villages. These villagers are known as *fellahin.* In the words of the French scholar, Henry Habib Ayrout, the *fellahin* are "the rural proletariat of Egypt."[5]

Since the days of the great nineteenth-century Egyptian liberator, Muhammed 'Ali, the *fellahin* have been glorified in literature and art. Their asceticism and patience, their disdain for mechanization, their successful survival through fifty centuries of poverty and deprivation, are the ingredients of a great romantic tradition. Henry Ayrout, who wears his admiration for the *fellahin* on his sleeve, declares, "From the beginnings of the Old Kingdom . . . they have changed their masters, their religion, their language and their crops but not their way of life."[6] Near the river Nile today, soil is still being carried in a basket, a practice that dates to the pharaonic period. The familiar scenes of buffalo and cow still pulling the iron-tipped, wooden plow have not disappeared. The traditional *saqiyeh* waterwheel and the *shadoof,* or long, counterweighted, wooden pole fastened to a leather water bucket, while far fewer than in the past, are still in evidence in the poorest villages on the banks of the Nile.

City dwellers in Egypt do not always share the misty vision of the noble peasant on the Nile. More often, they think of their countryfolk as boorish, devious, inscrutable, and incapable of reason. In an extreme view, opinion in the city might parallel that of the British colonialists who pronounced that the *fellahin* did not need education but instead should be taught civic virtue and better morals.[7]

Under a revisionist view held by political scientist, Timothy Mitchell, many of the stereotypes of the Egyptian *fellahin* have been scrutinized and overturned. It turns out that the peasant along the Nile is probably no more conservative or opposed to change than peasants elsewhere in the world.[8] Mechanization is gradually coming to Nile Valley agriculture. Artificial fertilizer often replaces the Ethiopian silt that now settles in Lake Nasser. There is an increasing number of tractors, reapers and threshers which have replaced labor of the ox and the buffalo. The *fellah* may indeed be a hidebound conservative shut off from change, but his capacity for hard work continues to be monumental and the *Qur'an* does not say that working seven days a week is unacceptable to God.

The one trait on which everyone would agree is the *fellah*'s dedication to the land. He is heir to a five-thousand-year-old culture of agriculture. The soil he so laboriously works is a vital part of his psyche, his strength and his vigorous good health. For the *fellahin* of Egypt, the threat of having to sell off one's land is the most dreaded of personal tragedies.

In common with most underdeveloped countries, land reform in Egypt has had limited success. Despite the nineteenth-century agrarian reforms of Muhammed 'Ali, the proportion of land held in large estates increased markedly in the nineteenth century. This intensified the prevailing exploitation of the peasant and produced, in part, the conditions of serfdom that led to the Nasser revolution in 1952. After Nasser removed the monarchy and the remnants of British control, he embarked on policies of breaking up large landholdings, transfers of property to the *fellahin,* expansion of irrigation to benefit small peasants, and the enactment of minimum wage laws. But these policies were only partially effective in easing the lives of those who worked the land. In 1980, 58 percent of the agricultural families in Egypt were still landless. In fact, the *fellah* has less acreage per capita than he did after Muhammed 'Ali wrested the land away from the Ottoman Turks. As a result, social and economic power in the villages still belongs to large property owners. In his book *Development and Social Change in Rural Egypt,*[9] Richard Adams notes the exalted status of the largest landowner in one district in Upper Egypt who lived in a three-story, colonial mansion with marble floors: "When he saunters through the community, *fellahin* women sometimes bow and kiss his hand before entreating him for a loan."

Egyptian villages along the Nile are composed of many small hamlets. There may be as many as twenty-five thousand people living within the boundaries of a village. Typically, villagers live in mud-brick houses which are remarkably cool in summer and hold the sun's warmth in winter. A sizable village will provide a police station, a government clinic or small hospital, and several government elementary schools. It will also have coffee houses, gas stations, food stores and many shops. Yet the Nile village continues to be a very simple rural community with no manufacturing except for small, local crafts.

Women are the bedrock of village life. Even in the intense heat of the summer months when sandstorms are a common occurrence, the peasant woman, in addition to her regular household duties, must go twice a day to the fields to cut fodder and haul it back to feed the family's buffalo, goats, geese, and chickens. Along the Nile, a woman's day begins before dawn. As the men go to sunrise prayers, the wife wakes the children, cooks breakfast, milks the buffalo, cleans the house, and washes the family clothes by hand at the local irrigation ditch. She makes cheese, washes the cooking pots, carries buckets of water home from the town pump or from the river, and makes dung cakes from buffalo manure and straw to fuel her brick oven. Several times a week, she bakes bread. At the end of the day, the wife prepares the evening meal and again washes the pots. The man works long hours in the fields, but he is the ''pasha'' and never helps the woman with chores.

Throughout Egypt and the Muslim world, most women are judged by whether they bear children, especially sons. But the reasons are economic as well as religious. It is vital for the couple to produce sons, both to care for them in their old age and to farm the family land today as well as later on when the father is no longer strong enough to work. The Egyptian proverb is ''You can only rely on your child descending from your loins and your calf from your cow.'' Since specific burial procedures are required of all Muslims, the *fellahin* also produce lots of children to make certain that someone will be around to give them a proper burial when they die. Many Egyptian families have eight, nine, or ten children, sometimes desperately trying for a son after the birth of many daughters. The mortality rate in Egypt is still very high. One out of three newborn babies in Upper Egypt dies in the first year. To be ensured that he will be survived by two sons, a man must sire seven or eight babies in his lifetime.

Birth control devices and information are available free at government dispensaries. Yet, in a country where the roots of Muslim fundamentalism run deep and many local religious sheikhs are unwilling to preach the virtues of contraception, the message is not adequately circulated to a superstitious and semi-literate people. With the patronizing attitude many urban rich hold toward the rural poor, the story is told in Cairo of one woman who had decided to adopt family planning. She complained that even though she fed her husband birth control pills every day, she still became pregnant.

Nevertheless, to share the crushing work load, the village family must also have daughters. Girl children, while not greeted at birth with the euphoric reception accorded to male babies, are necessary and welcome. In fact, families that produce no daughters frequently adopt very young girls. From the age of eight or nine and until she marries (sometimes before the legal Egyptian age of sixteen) the daughter in a peasant family will milk the buffalo, feed the animals, help with household chores and tend to the care of younger siblings, who tumble barefooted and barebottomed on the mud floor of the house. Egyptian mothers and daughters share an intense closeness and intimacy which may be strengthened by mutual discontent with their lot in life and further by the knowledge that the daughter will eventually leave home as a bride and take up residence in the family household of her husband. An old Arab proverb mourns: ''There is neither sister nor mother to share my misery.''

As in other parts of the world, unemployment and economic stagnation in the Egyptian valley cause migration. The *fellahin* do not move as families, yet millions of male peasants now leave Egypt to seek high-paying jobs in oil-producing countries such as Iraq and Saudi Arabia. Emigration is encouraged by the Egyptian government as a measure to reduce unemployment and to provide foreign exchange. In the late 1980's, annual remittances by Egyptian laborers abroad exceeded three billion dollars a year, next to tourism, the single largest source of hard currency. While this provides economic relief at home, the daily burden on the peasant wife and children has increased. Hence the *fellah's* wife is often the boss of the family, with total responsibility for directing work and husbanding the family's resources.

The High Dam at Aswan did more than revolutionize Egyptian agriculture. It also introduced electricity to the countryside, which, in turn, produced access to television, a most important break with village tradition. Tiny hamlets along the Nile now enjoy a bit of escapism and romance to break the tedium of village life. But there are only a smattering of television sets scattered throughout the drab clusters of little houses. Under a system of shared viewing, gatherings of neighbors become engrossed in old Egyptian films that vividly depict forbidden romance and deliver moralistic commentary on sinful life in the city. Both sexes particularly adore action movies from India, filled with swordplay, spilled blood, lustful passions, and murderous revenge.

Since the arrival of television, soccer has become an obsession with the sports-minded villagers. Small Egyptian boys in flannel pajamas sit transfixed before a flickering screen. They dream of becoming a Pelé or a Diego Maradona. Each hamlet has a soccer team which challenges teams from other hamlets along the river. Soccer champions in these "bush leagues" may, in turn, compete with teams from more distant villages. All of Egypt is captivated by the World Cup. It is watched by huge audiences who can't bear to leave their sets to wash pots or milk the buffalo or put the goats away for the night.

Oddly enough, it appears that television advertising has not made village women dissatisfied with their lot. Pictures of happy Cairo housewives smiling as they dump a particular soap powder into their glistening washing machines record an alien event that is just too far removed from village life on the Nile. In real life, hamlet dwellers have never seen such appliances, some of their houses have no indoor plumbing (in extremely poor villages there may be no town water spigot), and such odd contraptions would never fit into their small, mud-brick houses. These women do their washing communally, gossiping with neighbors as they squat next to the diesel pump which draws water into their irrigation ditches. In more advanced communities, the women carry pots of aluminum and tin instead of the older waterpots of clay.

For folklorists and ethnologists, the advent of television often puts an end to fertile sources of academic research. Once, each village had a local storyteller. For entertainment, illiterate peasants were dependent on public recitations. The local storyteller might be a weaver or a dyer or a farmer in the daytime, but after dark he became a spellbinder, transfixing his amusement-starved audience with a compelling narrative of romance and adventure. The audience, in turn, contributed small sums of money in exchange for his tales. In Egypt, many years ago, professional storytellers traveled from village to village and became main events in cafés and at folk-religious festivals and special celebrations. These epic storytellers would go on for days, recounting adventures from the past and narrating legends, I've been told, sometimes even longer than the *Iliad* and the *Odyssey* combined. With flamboyant gestures, they would embellish their colorful narrations, repeating tales handed down from great-grandfathers. A few of these storytellers exist but they play a much diminished role in village life. Peasants and sociologists alike blame television for the disappearance of these eloquent and esteemed orators. In fact, the orators' popularity was fading well before the advent of television.[10]

It is said that the soil breeds superstitions. Belief in hidden spirits is deeply embedded in the culture of Upper Egypt. In fertile villages along the Nile, superstitions have mainly to do with the birth and rearing of children. For Muslims generally, the color blue is held to be a protector. It is seen everywhere, from blue beads braided into a baby's hair to the blue domes of mosques reflecting the skies of heaven. The dominant threat is the Evil Eye. Many villagers paint their doors blue to ward off its powers. They may also dip their hands in paint or in blood and make five-fingered handprints on the walls of their houses as insurance against entry by the forces of evil. The handprint with fingers outstretched is also said to resemble the Arabic writing of Allah. The Evil Eye is blamed for a woman's milk drying up, for the death of water buffalos, and for human infertility.

Infertility is a most terrible curse upon a woman and superstition may dictate extreme remedies. In a contemporary book[11] in which five Egyptian women tell the stories of their lives, a village woman describes the way one childless woman removed a hex. She swabbed her breasts and stomach with water used to wash a corpse, then rinsed her mouth using the same water. The hex was then removed and she could—and did—become pregnant. In Upper Egypt, ancient, blue-glazed amulets in the shape of gods or sacred animals are frequently used to guarantee the birth of children. Women in villages step over these amulets seven times to ensure their fertility. Making a visit to such sites of antiquity as walled temples and pyramids is also considered, by some peasants, to be effective in promoting conception. In some villages of Upper Egypt, attaching a small piece of fox skin to the head of one's last living child is believed to guarantee the birth of still another baby.

It was reported in the early part of the twentieth century that, to prevent conception, a peasant woman might bury the stones of dates, hiding them in a wall of her house, first covering them with blood from the afterbirth of her last child. The number of date stones hidden in the wall would control the number of years she would have without another offspring.

Hair cuttings and nail parings are carefully saved in rural Egypt. If they were allowed to fall into the hands of malevolent strangers, injury could befall the original owners. In fact, the powers of human hair are of such potency, a man can win the love of a woman if he succeeds in obtaining some hair from her comb and hiring a local magician to turn it into a magical charm. She immediately succumbs to the magician's powers and falls madly in love with the suitor.

Egyptian peasants are firm believers in supernatural beings. First, there are *jinn,* who are usually good spirits and live underground. Then there are '*afrits* who also live underground in an organized society with a king at the head. They are made of fire and are connected with evil. When their fire is put out, they may take revenge unless the person extinguishing the fire forewarns the spirit with a suitable quotation from the *Qur'an.* These malign beings often appear in the form of an animal, such as a dog or cat.

If an individual becomes possessed by demons, a powerful village magician will be summoned to exorcise the evil spirit. Villagers also believe that both nightmares and sleepwalking are caused by '*afrits,* and if a peasant should drown in a canal, the spot where he entered the water is haunted. Therefore, one should never go alone to that spot on the water's edge because an '*afrit* will drag that person into the water. These spirits are also capable of kindly and helpful acts. In some villages, it is believed that an uncircumcised boy may be carried away by '*afrits* during the night. When the boy is brought back the same night, the mother will discover that he has been circumcised in an operation far superior to that performed by the village barber.

As in many Mediterranean societies, sexual purity in a woman, and the female modesty that protects it, are deeply venerated in Egypt. The finest compliment a young woman may receive is that she has *hishma,* or modesty. In the villages of Upper Egypt, young girls who have reputations as flirts or who engage in casual conversation with young men, may bring the deepest shame on their families. A woman's reputation may be destroyed by a mere rumor that she has associated with a man before marriage. A girl who has a reputation for unchastity may forfeit her chances of matrimony. It is the ultimate responsibility of the males in the family to protect their women from acts of immodesty. In some communities, the more conservative males in the family become enraged if a daughter or sister leaves the house without a proper head covering or veil.

In rural Egypt, men believe that the most serious threat to female modesty is that female sexual desires are, by nature, far more intense than men's. In some places it is believed that drinking water of the Nile as a child makes a girl passionate when she grows up.[12] Since the clitoris is identified as the center of female sexual drives, the "temptations" of women are curtailed by the practice of female circumcision, or clitoridectomy. Girls undergo the brutal procedure sometime between ages five and ten. While it is beginning to lose its hold even in rural areas, this custom is still widely practiced both in village communities and in the poorer sections of Cairo. Professor Diane Singerman describes the practice in Egypt: "Circumcision is seen as a rite of passage, which occurs before a girl reaches puberty and prepares a woman to engage in sexual relations when she marries."[13] There are gypsies for girls and barbers in the case of boys who specialize in the procedure but are not trained or licensed by the state. Because it has been customary for women to be circumcized, parents concerned about their daughters' chances of making good marriages are reluctant to be the first to abandon the practice. According to anthropologist Andrea Rugh, "women are highly involved in perpetuating this mutilation of female circumcision on one another. In fact, women are active participants in the exercise of most forms of social control over themselves."[14] Because this custom is deeply rooted in tradition and is considered an integral and necessary part of being fully prepared for marriage, the system is perpetuated.[15]

For the peasant woman in Egypt, marriage is an important rite of passage. Remaining single is never acceptable. Almost always, the marriage takes place between relatives, usually first cousins, and between a man and woman from the same village. Until she brings forth a child, the young bride's life is totally secluded. Marriage to a member of her mother's family offers the bride the comfort that, after the union, she will live close to her maternal roots, and thus be less lonely.

In rural villages, marriages based on love are almost unheard of. The marriage contract, called an *ittifaq*, is negotiated between the girl's father and the father of the prospective bridegroom. The boy and girl are never present. The boy's father pays a call at the house of the prospective bride and asks for the hand of the daughter. The usual phrase is *"talbeen al gurb,"* or "We wish to get closer to you." In due course, the marriage contract is signed by the two fathers.[16] The bride's price is set by negotiation. A down payment on the bride's price is delivered after the marriage document has been drawn. Using the down payment, the girl's parents shop for the trousseau. The written contract of marriage is religiously binding, and if either the bride or groom should die before the marriage day, the survivor is entitled to a share of the other's property. As soon as the other women in the girl's household learn of the marriage agreement (which doesn't take long, as houses are small and one can easily hear through walls), the women scurry around preparing as elaborate a celebration as they can muster up on short notice. They sing and utter cries of joy, trilling ululations of happiness. There follows a meal of celebration which ends with a reading from the Scripture and a prayer to God that the marriage will be successful and that the union will bring forth children.

Shortly thereafter, the two families agree upon the marriage date, usually several weeks in the future. This allows time for proper assembling of a dowry and for the groom to gather his gifts for the bride. Typically, the groom's family is obliged to buy clothing for other members of the bride's family. The girl's family procures the all-important set of furniture with which she will begin housekeeping in her new home. She must have a *tisht* (or washbasin), a round table, two copper pots, bedroom furniture, a new mattress, pillows, coverlets, a wardrobe, and a new sofa. Once assembled, the bride's new furniture is often loaded on a donkey cart and proudly paraded through the unpaved village streets. The bride's family may be hard pressed to finance these heavy expenditures, but it is essential that they dig up the necessary funds. They may sell a full-grown buffalo or a buffalo calf to pay for the furniture or they may choose to go heavily into debt. In a world where the male may easily and unilaterally rescind a marriage, it is essential that the bride be propertied and have a good start. If she should be divorced, her furniture and her jewelry will belong solely to her, and these possessions may represent her only financial security.

Two days before the marriage night, the bridegroom and some of his unmarried friends and relatives pass through the village inviting local friends and families to the wedding. The chosen invitees are expected to make small contributions of food or money. The couple wins prestige by having many guests. Almost indiscriminate invitations may be issued—even to enemies.

On the day before the wedding, the bride embarks on a ceremonial walk to the Nile with unmarried female friends of her own age. They must return before sunset, their jars filled with river water. After the river visit, friends and female relatives prepare the bride for the ceremony. She is bathed and perfumed. All of her body hair is removed. The shaving of the body is a purification ritual that has been observed in Egypt since pharaonic times. Henna, a powder ground from the Egyptian privet plant, is applied to her hands and feet. Henna is considered an emblem of purity and is used throughout the Arab world by women of every social class. Mixed with water, the henna becomes an orangy-red paste. For effective hand staining, a ball of henna is placed in the palm. The hand is tightly bound overnight with a linen cloth. On the morning of the wedding day, the bandage is removed and the bright orange color remains on the skin for many days. The female relatives now excitedly lay out the bride's new clothes and her glittering gold jewelry. Her unmarried friends pinch her thighs in order to share her good luck. As the women bustle about the bride preparing her for her wedding, they sing a song of erotic double entendre.

> How pretty is the one we are entertaining,
> How we are admiring her.
> The snake in his hole
> has spent a sleepless night
> He kept one eye on her forehead,
> and the other on her ankles.

On the evening before the wedding, the groom, too, has had a bath at the home of his closest friend. He is dressed in an elegant *galabiyyah*, a turban, and he sometimes wears a sword or dagger. His hands, too, are dyed with henna. Next comes the groom's torchlit evening procession around the village. There are celebratory gunshots and the women throw salt on the wedding party. Sweetmeats and dates are distributed to children. After the call of the *muezzin*, the men enter the mosque for evening prayer.

On the long awaited wedding day, the bridegroom, accompanied by his kinsmen and young friends, proceed through the town, beating tambourines and cymbals. They are leading a camel loaded with wheat, beans and lentils. A mock fight to claim ownership of the camel may take place between the bridegroom's and the bride's male relatives, each side shouting "The camel is ours." The camel will remain at the bride's house until the newlyweds set up housekeeping. The supplies loaded on the camel's back will provide the couple with enough dry food to last for three months. Finally, the groom and his friends arrive at the bride's house and the bride, fully veiled, shyly comes out of the house with her male relatives to greet the groom.

In very old-fashioned villages, a ceremonial defloration (*a la baladi* or "the folk way"), while a dying custom, may still take place at the bride's house in full view of both the midwife and female relatives. In some villages, a ceremonial defloration song is sung outside the room while the defloration is taking place.[17]

> Behold the blood of the peasant girl
> Behold, it's red and bright like an apple.
> On an aluminum bed, whether you cry or not
> This is a night worth the world.
> On a bed made of brass, whether you cry or not
> Consider it a night among nights:
> It will soon be over.
> On bedsheets made of silk, O Bride give me a kiss.
> O Bridegroom, the night is long.
> On a mat of straw, O Bride give me a kiss.
> O Bridegroom, long live your people.

The midwife stains cloths providing proof of the bride's virginity. In the streets, rifles are fired and drums beat, cymbals ring out as the world learns that the bride is pure. Then the groom goes off with his friends to feast on roast lamb, seemingly in no hurry to begin married life with his bride. In modern Egypt, more and more couples are consummating their union in private (*a la frangi*, or the French or European way), without the embarrassment of observed defloration. Four days later, the actual consummation of the union takes place, after which the bride remains a virtual prisoner. Secluded for days in the groom's house, she is allowed to see only the groom's female relatives.

In the villages, a woman's great gift is her fertility. She does not think of herself as a sexual partner but as the mother of men. It is universally expected that the new bride will become pregnant almost immediately, for it is through childbearing that she will attain her proper social status. A skillful, new bride who wishes to avoid divorce will seek to please her husband by slavishly obeying her mother-in-law. If a man loses interest in his bride or takes a fancy to another woman and therefore decides on divorce, he repeats "I divorce you" three times. With these words the divorce, or *talaaq,* is final. But the *fellah* on the Nile rarely uses the *Qur'anic* privilege of divorce. The cost of maintenance and returned goods is just too high.

Life in the Nile Valley is a story of illiteracy, crushing poverty, hard work, superstition and traditionalism. But the powerful and pervasive force in life is religion. Islam tells its believers precisely how to live and what to do. Appealing to the deep human yearning for certitude, it lays down, for forty-five million Egyptians and a billion or more other Muslims throughout the world, five "pillars" or obligatory duties. These injunctions are known as the five pillars of Islam.

The first pillar is the creed or profession of faith, "There is no god but Allah, and Muhammed is His Prophet." The second pillar is the *salaat* or required prayer five times a day—upon rising, at noon, in mid-afternoon, at sunset, and before retiring. The first prayers of the day must be performed as the first, faint light of dawn breaks over cities and hamlets. The rooster crows and the *muezzin* at the village mosque summons the faithful over loud-speakers. He calls, "God is great! God is great!" In the morning he adds, "Prayer is better than sleep." Women usually pray at home. Men go to a local mosque if one is nearby, but Muslim prayers performed anywhere are acceptable. As one travels through Upper Egypt, it is common to see a farmer or truck driver stopped by the side of the road or at the edge of a field. He washes himself, faces toward Mecca, and slips to his knees with his hands and face to the ground. His shoes are always removed. The third pillar of Islam is *zakaat* or alms giving. Islamic law requires everyone except the indigent to give a percentage of his wealth to orphans, the clergy and the homeless.

The two most visible pillars of Islam are the observance of Ramadan and the performance of the *Hajj,* or pilgrimage to Mecca. Ramadan is the annual celebration of the month in which the *Qur'an* was revealed to the Prophet. At the start of Ramadan, the mosques are lit with lanterns. Colored Ramadan lights and paper streamers decorate the streets. During Ramadan, Muslims may not smoke, eat, drink or have sexual intercourse during daytime hours. Only the sick, the pregnant, the traveler, and those fighting a holy war are excused. Because the Islamic calendar is based on lunar months, Ramadan changes dates each year and moves through the seasons. The abstinence from taking in food and water is most punishing when the holy month falls in the midst of a scorching Egyptian summer. As dusk falls each evening during Ramadan, a cannon is fired ending the daily fast. Muslim families gather to share an evening meal which is usually more sumptuous than any normal dinner. Among the upper classes, the nighttime repast may sometimes be bountiful enough to be described as gluttonous. Strict Muslims believe that the entire purpose of Ramadan fasting—to build self-discipline and the control of appetites—has been lost as at sunset many Egyptian Muslims take to the streets and cafés to indulge in social activities and celebration. But fasting always begins once more at dawn, technically defined as that point in time when the human eye can distinguish between a black and white thread.

In Cairo, the end of the holy month is announced by the firing of twenty shots from a cannon at the Citadel. Villagers in Upper Egypt gather around radios waiting for the official word announcing that the sheikhs have sighted the sliver of a new moon. The feast that follows the end of Ramadan is the *Eid al-Fitr,* or Festival of Breaking the Fast. This is an important feast. Families read from the *Qur'an* and extra prayers are read in the mosques. The first day of the feast, men visit the cemeteries. On the second day, women and children walk to the graveyards, carrying picnics and honoring the graves of their relatives. A great deal of visiting takes place between families and friends. Women bake special kinds of date-paste and butter cookies sprinkled with sugar. Sixty days later comes the great Feast of the Sacrifice, commemorating the sacrifice of Abraham and lasting for three days. Sheep are slaughtered. Anwar Sadat's widow, Jehan Sadat, notes that during this period of feasting "it was unlawful *not* to eat."[18]

The final pillar of Islam is the *Hajj,* or religious pilgrimage to Mecca and Mt. 'Arafaat, the holy sites of the Arabian peninsula. This sacred journey is obligatory at least once in a lifetime for any Muslim whose health and financial means permit. The *Hajj* requirement is not absolute but most Muslims expect, and seriously intend, to perform it. Poor peasants often save all their lives to pay for the pilgrimage, putting aside bits of money in a *Hajj* box. Before the ritual of the *Hajj* is performed, the pilgrim is duty bound to repay debts, give back anything he has stolen, repent of his sins and provide for his family lest he die during the voyage.

Over the centuries, an elaborate infrastructure was needed to supply thousands of pilgrims with food, water and supplies for the long journey. The enormous caravans that made the twelve-hundred-mile voyage across the desert from Cairo to Mecca were often described as moving cities. They contained thousands of pack animals loaded with grain, water and cooking oil. Blacksmiths, protective guards and sandalmakers accompanied the pilgrims.

The *Hajj* has long been commercially important as well as a religious event. Many pilgrims doubled as spice sellers, silk traders, dealers in ivory, gold, sandalwood and ostrich feathers. The return voyage to Egypt was accomplished with immense swaying and lurching camel caravans heavily laden with spices, frankincense, aloe wood, and silks acquired in Mecca from eastern merchants who had journeyed there from India and Samarkand. The historian S. D. Goitein recounts the standing wish of a Muslim pilgrim: "May your *Hajj* be accepted, your sin forgiven, and your merchandise not remain unsold."[19]

The *Hajj* has always attracted the elderly and the sick. An aged Muslim pilgrim often carried his grave linens with him. In anticipation of imminent death, he performed the ritual ablutions with water, or simply with sand or dust. He then scratched a trench in the desert, covered himself with sand and said his final prayers, with the sure knowledge that the wind would soon cover his grave forever. Many caravans from Mecca left behind the corpses of dead camels buried along with the graves of infirm pilgrims who succumbed to heatstroke or heart attacks. Family members who traveled out into the desert to meet relatives were often greeted with grisly tidings that a loved one had contracted a dread disease or had even been murdered by marauding Bedouin. Their happy anticipations of reunion changed to sorrowful wailings of grief when the bereaved realized that their father or brother would remain forever in an unmarked grave, obliterated by desert sands.

Advance riders used to race ahead of the caravans spreading joyous and long-awaited news that pilgrims were finally returning. It was a Muslim tradition that the pilgrims' families would decorate the facades of their homes with naive drawings of the travelers and images of the camels and ships on which they made their way. Verses from the *Qur'an* embellished the artists' renderings and often framed doorways and windows. The wall paintings also depicted the great mosque at Mecca and the *Ka'ba,* its most sacred shrine. Even today, charming new and old renditions of Egyptian folk art depicting the *Hajj* may be seen on village walls throughout the Nile Valley.

Airplane travel today has dramatically altered the accessibility of the *Hajj.* The vision of the four golden minarets of the sacred mosque at Mecca is thrust upon the pilgrim with too much speed. The pilgrim no longer approaches Mecca on foot or on camelback, slowly savoring the sacred images in his mind's eye. Moreover, since the mid-nineteen-fifties, the ease of air travel to Mecca has exponentially increased the numbers of pilgrims who go each year. With *Hajj* pilgrims now reaching two million a year, each Muslim country is now assigned a quota of permitted travelers. The pressure on facilities in Mecca is enormous since there is only one period a year, the first ten days of the month of *Dhu'l-Hijjah,* in which the *Hajj* obligation may be fulfilled.

A hopeful pilgrim applies to a branch of Egypt's Pilgrimage Commission. A few weeks before the

Hajj begins, the lucky applicant receives a postcard saying: "Congratulations. You have been chosen to go on the *Hajj!*" Priority is usually given to older people and to those who had a very difficult time raising the money. Saudi Arabian facilitators arrange everything for the traveler. Among Muslims as far away as Jersey City, New Jersey, discussions have arisen regarding the use of a credit card to "charge your *Hajj.*" Islamic law strictly forbids paying interest or usury of any kind.

On the pilgrimage to Mecca, rich and poor are equal in the sight of God. After first performing nine ritual ablutions, trimming beards, and cutting nails and hair, men and women alike don their simple, pilgrim robe. Only leather sandals may be worn during the ritual observances. The first major ritual in the holy city is the making of seven circumambulations of the *Ka'ba,* "the holy house of God," in whose wall is embedded the sacred Black Stone, said to be a meteorite which fell from heaven. The circumambulation is performed at the beginning and the end of the pilgrimage. Next, the pilgrim visits the shrine of Abraham who is believed to be the originator of the *Hajj.* This is followed by a trip to the sacred well of Zam-Zam whose waters are said to possess mystical powers. Then, the faithful travel three miles from Mecca to Mina, a small village where Muhammed passed the night on his last pilgrimage. The next day, the pilgrims walk to Mt. 'Arafaat, twelve miles southwest of Mecca, the sacred ground where the penitent stand before God and receive his forgiveness. The walk to Mt. 'Arafaat is the most requisite and central rite of the *Hajj.* On the return journey to Mina, there is a ceremony called "stoning the devils." Each pilgrim collects forty-nine pebbles and casts them at a stone pillar which symbolizes the evil forces in the world. After the stoning, a blood sacrifice is offered in the form of sheep, goat, or camel meat. Because of the huge numbers of *Hajj* pilgrims, it is impossible to distribute the sacrificial meat to the poor as was originally intended. In a bow to modernity and mass production, food packaging plants have been built to provide later distribution of the sacrificial meat.

The pilgrims return to Mecca no later than the thirteenth day of the month and make the farewell circumambulation of the *Ka'ba.* They are now ready to return to the profane world. According to early nineteenth-century accounts, the pilgrims returned bringing flasks of water from the sacred well, dust from the Prophet's tomb, frankincense, combs and rosaries of aloeswood. Today, as in past centuries, the pilgrims return home with a sense of inner peace and a feeling of religious tranquillity. Those who have made the pilgrimage are called *Hajji.* They are presented with a certificate attesting to the fact they have performed the sacred journey.

In Egypt it is said "death is a black camel who comes to everyone's door." The nineteenth-century British Arabist-ethnologist, E.W. Lane, describes the lamentations of the bereaved wife, "Oh my master, oh my camel" (he who has provided and carried the burden), "Oh my lion," "Oh my resource!" "Oh my misfortune." As soon as news of death has traveled through a village, female relatives as well as professional mourners run through the village wailing and screaming. They praise the fine qualities of the deceased. They reproach God for taking him away. With faces painted black or blue, they continue their plaintive cries for hours until hoarse from their exertions.[20]

Muslims bury their dead promptly, within twelve hours after death. The body is washed with warm water and soap, always by a member of the same sex. This ablution confers a state of purity upon the departed. The body's orifices are stuffed with cotton wool. Then it is sprinkled with water mixed with camphor, then rose water. The corpse is wrapped in a winding cloth and covered lastly with a green shawl. In Upper Egyptian villages, an animal, preferably a ram, must be sacrificed on the exact spot where death occurred. If the family is poor and cannot afford a ram, a goat will do. After the ceremony, the animal's meat will be given to the poor. The sacrificial blood spilling of the animal will insure that the soul goes to heaven.

Four men carry the corpse on a flat, wooden bier, wending their way through the narrow, dirt streets. On the way to the grave, the bearers may exchange places with neighbors who will take a turn in the burial procession. Carrying the dead is regarded as a pious act. Black-robed females walk behind the bier.

Some are bereaved relatives but, once again, there are others who are professional mourners. Both family and professionals raise their voices, wailing and ululating with grief, often bordering on hysteria. This burial custom that calls for extreme public wailing, breast-beating and often rending the garments, is an ancient one. It is frequently illustrated in carvings and paintings in pharaonic burial chambers.

In Egypt, as in the West, a burial plot is often bought and a tombstone erected long before it is needed. After death occurs, a burial permit is issued. The body will be positioned in a shallow grave with its head pointing toward the west so that the departed looks east toward Mecca. The day after a burial, female relatives of the deceased gather by his house and perform a slow dance of lamentation, tying a rope girdle around their waists, holding green, blue, and purple handkerchiefs. They scream and yell and beat their breasts. Others wail and sway and fall into each other's arms. Their faces, hands, and forearms are often stained with a blue indigo dye. During the period of mourning, family members sit speechless and motionless, often for weeks.

Alluvial fields are too valuable as agricultural land to be used for burial. Gravesites are positioned on the edge of the desert. On Fridays, peasant folk visit the cemeteries believing that on saints' birthdays and on the Muslim Sabbath, the souls of the dead temporarily return to the graves and wait at the cemetery to greet their relatives. Small, green birds, sometimes seen near graves, are believed to be the souls of the deceased.

The Temples and Tombs of Thebes

Nowhere in Egypt is there grandeur to compare with the temples and colossal statues of Luxor. Settled on the East Bank of the Nile before 2700 B.C., Luxor is the site of Homer's "hundred gated Thebes." It is the home of the majestic Temple of Karnak with its great hypostyle hall outlined by 134 massive columns, the tallest, nearly seventy feet high. Alexander the Great, who conquered Luxor in 332 B.C., added to the Temples of Karnak and Luxor. The emperors of Rome were worshipped at Luxor Temple until the sixth century A.D. Here, archeologists from around the world continue to explore the most lavish and brilliant period in the history of Egypt. Today, it is the tourist trade that makes Luxor rich. Towering hotels jam the corniche. Tourist shops offer "tomb treasures" of bluestone ibises, carved baboons, statues of Anubis (the black jackal of death), and miles of plaster scarabs. Dresses decorated with sequined heads of pharaohs tempt the shopper, as do golden slippers with turned-up toes and grinning, balsa wood crocodiles, painted a vivid yellow with black spots.

Elaborately ornamented, shiny, black, horse-drawn carriages ferry the tourists and local citizens around town. On the outside of these caleches are photographs of Egyptian film stars embellished with brass amulets in the form of five-fingered hands with gold and silver trim. The most resourceful drivers always ask for a little extra *baksheesh* "for the horse."

Luxor has no industry. The surrounding area on the east bank is agricultural, and only a few miles inland from the Nile, one would never even know that close by there were Sheraton and Hilton Hotels, a Club Med, and armies of tourists laden with cameras and Baedekers. In the back streets of Luxor, town dwellers and transplanted peasants live a simple, village-style life, occasionally enriched by the wages of a family member who may have had the good fortune to obtain a service job at a nearby hotel. A family so blessed can count on about fifty dollars a month in extra cash. Despite the booming tourist trade, hotel jobs are not easy to find. Most townsfolk in Luxor eke out the same sparse farming existence as other villagers along the Nile.

My favorite photographic route in Luxor—one I took many times—was the southern spur of the Avenue of Sphinxes which winds its way from the tenth pylon at Karnak Temple to Luxor Temple, two miles to the south. Along this meandering avenue of headless stone beasts, there are over seven hundred crouching sphinx statues. The avenue of statues leads away from Karnak's majesty, finally to the back streets of Luxor, and then into Zeniya, a welter of human activity. Here it becomes clear that Luxor is really a rural village masquerading as a small city. As I walked, old men and women sat in the pale, January sunshine, tending grandchildren, holding small animals, or just basking in the warmth of the winter sun. The women's heads were covered with black headcloths but their faces remained uncovered. A female baker flattened perfect rounds of unleavened dough on long-handled wooden boards; a man on a donkey-pulled wagon drove from house to house, crying out that he was selling poultry. Stacked cages of white chickens bounced and flapped behind him. Marked by his giant, silver cauldron glistening in the sun, one Luxor citizen was the proprietor of a fast food stand. In his pot was *fuul mudammes,* a staple of the Egyptian diet. *Fuul* is a paste of fava beans, boiled overnight in an earthen vessel and eaten on pita bread with linseed oil, butter, or lime juice.

A middle-aged woman smiled at me. She sold lovely clay pots, the color of her wrinkled skin. I quickly dismissed the thought of shipping a carton of this inexpensive, but highly breakable, cookware home to the United States. At the edge of town, the insignia of ancient Egypt reappeared. In a green field was a wooden waterwheel slowly turned by a blindfolded brown-and-white ox. The animal was driven by a stooped, old man who wore only a loincloth tied below his waist. His chest was ribbed like a washboard. The wheel's jugs spilled water into the farmer's irrigation ditches, raising the water level in the same manner as it had been done under the Pharaohs.

One afternoon in Luxor, I accepted a gracious invitation to tea with Helen and Jean Jaquet in their small and simply designed house, uniquely located, quite literally, on the walls of the majestic Temple of Karnak. Jean is a Swiss-born architectural historian and Helen is an American Egyptologist. The Jacquets, who make their winter home in Luxor, return each November to their house on the Karnak wall.

The Karnak Temple complex is also home to a pack of half-wild, half-domesticated Egyptian dogs. These yellow, short-haired, pointy-eared creatures look much like the dogs of Thailand and Indonesia. They roam the vast temple enclosure and scavenge for food. Each fall, the Jacquets adopt a few more of these dogs as pets. Those chosen soon grow accustomed to their sleepy life of pampered ease atop the temple wall, from which vantage point they smugly bark at less fortunate dogs in the ruins below. When the Jacquets leave for home each year in the spring, the dogs return to their semi-wild scavenging companions. Occasionally, the officials of Luxor pronounce that the feral dog population has grown too large and a mass rifle execution is carried out by the Luxor police.

From an observation post above the temple enclosure, we could see all four gates of Karnak. Listening to the distant call of the *muezzin* announcing sunset prayers, we watched a fiery, January sun slip quickly behind the giant pylons and obelisks. Erected 3,500 years ago and soaring ninety-seven feet high, Queen Hatshepsut's obelisk was silhouetted against a sky that was changing from orange to gold. In ancient times, people believed the stone shafts of obelisks were sacred and represented a form of the sun. The sky turned purple and, as we descended, it changed to the deep blue of a clear and star-filled Egyptian night.

For more than 2,000 years, from 2050 B.C. to the Roman conquest in 30 B.C., Luxor was the primary religious center of the pharaonic world. During the New Kingdom, Luxor Temple and its neighboring temple complex, Karnak, two miles to the north, were the most holy monuments of the god Amun-Re. Built on the old flood plain of the mighty Nile, Luxor Temple stands majestically in the center of Luxor town. Its towering colonnades come into view as one approaches the city by Nile river boat. Today, throughout the Nile Valley, water-borne salts are permeating the stone foundations of ancient structures. In Luxor, encrustations of salt are destroying the building stones of Karnak and Luxor temples. Ancient paintings, inscriptions and decorated surfaces photographed forty or fifty years ago have now all but disappeared. The culprit is the capillary action that pulls the salts out of the earth and up through the porous stones of the monuments. There appears to be no solution to the inexorable deterioration of monuments.

The Aswan High Dam has provided a controlled inundation of the Nile waters. Farmers are no longer dependent on the vicissitudes of seasonal droughts and uncertain flooding. Yet, the new dam has raised the level of the brackish ground water. In Luxor, a team of photographers, artists, and Egyptologists is working frantically to document these images before they disappear forever.

On the corniche at Luxor, hidden behind enormous metal gates and high walls covered with purple bougainvillea, stands a quiet oasis of scholarship. This is Chicago House, a graceful complex of sheltering stucco arches and sunny courtyards, a center of research and a haven of tranquillity among the bustle of horse-drawn carriages and frenetic tourists who clamber in and out of their docked river boats. Built in 1931 with Rockefeller funding, Chicago House, the Egyptian headquarters of the University of Chicago, is dedicated to a complicated epigraphic survey of temples and tombs in the Theban area. Egyptologist, Dr. Lanny Bell, director of Chicago House from 1977–1989, invited me and my companions to use the research institution as a place to study and share meals during my 1989 visit to Luxor. Dr. Bell is a person of profound scholarship and sensitivity, much beloved by everyone in Luxor from archeologists to Egyptian workmen. Chicago House grows its own lettuce and vegetables and has its own private well. It is reported to be the only place in Upper Egypt where a foreigner can eat a salad without regretting he has done so.

One cool, sunny, January morning, I was sitting in the high-ceilinged library at Chicago House, surrounded by piles of books written by nineteenth- and early twentieth-century British travelers to Egypt. In the quiet of this serene book-lined room, I was taking notes on discoveries that had taken place a hundred years earlier. A member of the Epigraphic Survey team entered the library and announced that a momentous event was taking place in the Sun Court of Luxor Temple. Egyptian conservators had been taking soil borings to determine the amount of minerals and salts in the earth below the Temple when their instruments suddenly struck a hard surface. They began to dig carefully with small hoes, finally unearthing a new treasure. They uncovered a buried cache of five pharaonic figures that had been hidden by either Egyptian priests or Roman soldiers at the end of the fourth century A.D. when Luxor Temple was converted into both a Roman camp for military troops and a cult place of the divine Roman emperors. Interestingly, the Romans did not destroy the holy figures from pharaonic times but merely covered them with earth, where they remained protected for sixteen hundred years.

On hearing news of this remarkable find, and eager to be a witness to the making of archeological history, I raced up the corniche from Chicago House to Luxor Temple, a mile to the south. Such excitement! By the time I arrived breathlessly at the Temple, I discovered to my great dismay that archeological guards had just patted the last shovelful of dirt over the bodies of the figures. Fearful that harm might befall them before Egypt's most illustrious experts could study and document the astonishing find, the earth of the Sun Court had been replaced over them. Sadly, I had missed a first glimpse of an oversized figure of Amenhotep III shown carrying a document case containing, perhaps, the deed to the temple. Now in a special warehouse in Luxor, this and the four other figures are currently being documented and studied by members of the Egyptian Antiquities Organization. Someday the figures will be on display in the Luxor Museum for the general public. But in Egypt, bureaucratic procedures move slowly. Zahi Hawass, archeological director of the area surrounding the Giza Pyramids outside Cairo, once speculated that perhaps only 30 percent of all treasures of Egyptian antiquity have been located and excavated.

Dr. Bell took us on a private tour of Luxor Temple, explaining that, uniquely in this temple, more than three thousand years of religious history are found in one place. Luxor Temple contains an eighth-century Christian church, a thirteenth-century Islamic mosque, and a pharaonic temple whose construction began over thirty-three hundred years ago. The present Temple was built by Amenhotep III and Ramses II and was dedicated to the Sun God, Amun-Re, and to the Royal Ka. The "Royal Ka" refers to a celebration of the unity of the earthly Egyptian monarch and the Divinity. At the time of coronation, each successor monarch slipped into the shoes of the prior king. A divine spark then entered the Pharaoh. Man and God became one as the mantle of kingship was passed on.

At Luxor there is no bridge across the Nile, but there are two classes of ferries. One is for the tourists who need to cross the river from their cruise boats or hotels in Luxor to visit western Thebes and the Valley of the Kings and its buried treasures. The other boat, the People's Ferry, is for the Egyptians who ride across the Nile to do business or visit relatives in the villages on the West Bank. To feel the human pulse of rural Egypt, I joined the throngs of Egyptians on the People's Ferry. Battered but seaworthy, this small double-decker boat plies the muddy Nile currents, cutting through stems of water hyacinths and floating debris to disgorge its load of Egyptians on both banks of the river.

Tuesday is market day in Luxor. On the Tuesday in January when I first ventured onto the People's Ferry, it was jammed and bustling. The entire noisy, turbulent and colorful world of rural Egypt seemed to be on board. I plunged into the crowds of turbanned men clad in blue or green *galabiyyahs* shouldering wooden cages of roosters and hoisting giant crates of cabbages, tomatoes, and melons. Mothers, covered from head to toe in black overdresses and modesty cloths, clutched their children protectively, and uneasily turned their faces away from the scrutiny of the few foreigners on board.

The cargo, which ranged from sacks of commercial fertilizer and machine parts to huge wooden masts for *felucca* boats of the Nile, lay stacked on the deck. Bales of alfalfa tied with rags, were piled near the boat's railing. The extraordinary vividness of alfalfa green is always startling. It seems to mirror the green of the Emerald City of Oz in all of its technicolor.

On the open main deck of this sturdy but creaking and rusty craft, children hawked paper cones filled with candy dyed an unappetizing, shocking pink. Vendors proffered cooked beans. Sweets and potato chips were for sale on makeshift tables. A small Egyptian boy tugged at one end of a frayed rope; tethered to the other end was a fat, cream-colored sheep. Lounging on a wooden bench against the boat's railing, an elderly man exhibiting a mouthful of rotted teeth munched contentedly on the end of a pale green stalk of sugar cane that must have been four feet long. Relatives from scattered hamlets greeted each other affectionately, apparently exchanging gossip about engagements and new grandchildren. The ferry became a floating theater of family reunion and sociability.

By custom, the upper deck of the People's Ferry is the exclusive domain of male passengers. They joked, smoked and gossiped, visibly sorry when the short ride came to an end. A few daredevil male Egyptians made the trip hanging out over the water with only one arm engaging the outside railing. In a spectacular feat of Egyptian derring-do, they allowed their cotton robes to billow in the wind like spinnakers, tempting fate that the boat might lurch and hurl them into the muddy swirls and eddies of the river twenty feet below.

As the golden cliffs of the West Bank grew closer, the motors of the ferry slowed. We were now approaching the little village of Gurna, the home of the Gurnawis who are said to be descendants of medieval tomb robbers. It is rumored that the Gurnawis still know about, and continue secretly to despoil, tombs on the West Bank that are as yet unknown to Egyptian authorities. Before the craft could be safely secured at the quai, a group of young males on board, wearing leather jackets and mounted on motor bikes, revved up their engines in the very midst of the village folk who tried to move clear of the exhaust and who expressed glaring disapproval at the raucous, bad manners of the irreverent young bucks. The river's level was unusually low and the bikers roared off the boat, their cycles completing acrobatic flying leaps through the air and then landing safely on the pier above.

We disembarked among the crowds of Egyptian passengers. The dust stirred up by the motor bikes was still swirling on the dirt-covered banks of the river. It was early in the day and the morning was still cool. We saw children riding donkeys to the fields. The Egyptian passengers quickly disappeared into the dust and mud streets of the village of Gurna. They paid no heed to the lure of the pharaonic burial grounds in the Valley of the Kings that lie hidden in the golden cliffs only a few miles ahead. Meantime, at another ferry landing a half mile north, bull horns summoned hundreds of foreigners from the tourist ferry to the streamlined, air-conditioned busses that awaited them.

In the past few days, these travelers had made exhausting visits to Aswan High Dam, Abu Simbel and the Tomb of Tutankhamun. They had taken the long boat cruise to Philae and a *felucca* ride on the Nile. Making their way toward the Valley of the Queens, they passed the great, seated, sandstone figures of Amenhotep III, known as the Colossi of Memnon. These crumbling, faceless statues once sat in front of the mortuary temple of the Pharaoh. The temple has long since collapsed and disappeared. Now, the statues look strangely out of place in the middle of an open plain. Sheep and goats graze close by and neighboring fields are planted with crops. In 1850, Florence Nightingale described the Colossi in a letter from Egypt written home to England. "They are such sightless, shapeless ruins, they look like sightless Lear after the storm—as if the lightning of heaven had rested upon them and made them the awful ruins you see."[21]

Now, in a climactic finale to their tour of Egypt, the travelers would make their tired march across the ochre-colored hills of Thebes to the secret, underground burial chambers of the Pharaohs and to the majestic, funerary temples of Ramses and Hatshepsut. I revelled in my chance to travel leisurely and to savor them all once again at my own pace.

A Country Circus

Sixty-five miles north of Aswan is the river town of Edfu. Travelers stop at Edfu because it is the home of the most completely preserved Ptolemaic temple in all of Egypt. After the shops close and the tourists return to their floating hotels, the Temple of Horus is deserted, and the granite statue of the falcon god, Horus, stands alone in front of the great Pylons. Edfu is a shuttered town. Only coffee houses and small tobacco shops remain open.

One cool, sunny, February afternoon, our antiquated river boat, the *Prince du Nil* (an inappropriate name because it demonstrably lacked any connection with royalty), chugged up river in the direction of Aswan. We came to a stop on a wide, stepped quai at Edfu, designed to be a landing place spacious enough to accommodate fifty river boats at one time. In the distance, at the top of the steep river bank, I spied a cluster of what looked to be canvas tents. On closer inspection, a large sideshow tent and a tattered big top flying the Egyptian flag came clearly into view.

A small, traveling circus was visiting Edfu. Scattered on the circus grounds was an array of games: ring toss, games to measure one's strength, and shooting galleries. The prizes were soft drinks, Kleenex, and cigarettes. A small merry-go-round was propelled by the tireless efforts of one solitary man who trotted, breathing hard, as he ran in a circle, chasing the platform which held seven, old-fashioned, painted, wooden horses with curling red lips, exposed, painted wooden tongues, and huge, shining white teeth. The contraption creaked and turned under his propulsion to the delight of a handful of small riders.

A vividly colored sideshow advertisement showed hands of playing cards and rabbits in hats, but the principal illustrations were a woman with a human head and serpent body, a second woman made of fire and electricity, and a magician named Chico Bico. As at sideshows everywhere, there was a gang of teenage boys taking turns peeping through a jagged tear in the canvas. This Egyptian knot-hole gang hoped to get a free look at the mysterious coils of the serpent woman who had been advertised outside in a most graphic and tantalizing manner. We decided that an Egyptian sideshow was worth a look. Unfortunately, the snake woman must have been on her lunch break. I wondered if her serpent's diet included mice and other small rodents. I soon realized, as we sat on the front row of backless, wooden benches, that a special sideshow performance was being staged for our benefit. The electric woman, who had jet black hair and Cleopatra bangs, was wearing a white silk robe covered with shimmering sequins. She held a long, fluorescent tube in one hand and she stepped daintily, one bare foot at a time, into a galvanized water basin. Her male partner, whom we took to be the highly touted Chico Bico, twirled around her Svengali-like. He touched the other end of her fluorescent tube. Magically, it began to glow with an intense bluish light. We applauded vigorously.

The second and final act of the abbreviated matineé version of the Edfu sideshow starred our same lady of fire and electricity. She lay with her eyes closed on a satin-covered bier, feigning unconsciousness or death. Chico Bico passed hoops over her bier, grinning at us conspiratorially as he demonstrated beyond the shadow of a doubt that there were no invisible wires suspending the electric woman from the roof of the tent. He tapped three times with a black wand on the side of her bier. Again, like magic, the satin bier began to rise from the small stage and to float through the air. Chico Bico took a deep bow while the sleeping fire and electricity woman floated four feet above the small wooden stage. The spectacle had ended.

That night after dinner on the *Prince du Nil*, we raced back up the hill to catch the first evening performance of the Edfu circus. Special seats had been reserved for us on the center section of bleachers. Young men with trays and aprons offered an unappetizing choice of pink corn candy or turquoise crackerjacks in paper cones.

To our left was a large bleacher section. Perched there were several hundred Egyptian men, clothed in white turbans and blue or tan *galabiyyahs*. They formed a solid masculine block, uninterrupted by any female form. A hundred pairs of dark eyes stared curiously in our direction. A few of the tourists had unintentionally exposed a few inches of their white shins.

To our right sat a section of well-dressed Egyptian families, mothers and grandmothers, garbed in expensive, floor-length dresses. They were wearing Islamic headdress and holding small children by the hands. These families, so beautifully clothed, must have been among Edfu's wealthiest and leading families. A few Egyptian men, some of them wearing western trousers and shirts, sat with their women in the choice boxes. Tinny, old-fashioned Barnum and Bailey circus music blasted out over two loudspeakers.

The performance had begun. First came four tumbler clowns. They wore baggy pants and oversized clown shoes. Their noses were covered by bulbous, cherry-red, clown noses and classic, bald-headed, clown wigs. They went through a tedious series of gyrations and gymnastic feats which involved springing up and down on trampolines, catching each other with their large clown feet, pedaling each other in the air with their feet and legs, and leapfrogging over one another. These gymnastic vaudevillians executed their routines to the accompaniment of a number of crude noises and sounds explicitly resembling breaking wind. This was met by howls of laughter from the turbanned males in the left bleachers. The gymnasts left the ring. Only the fattest clown remained. He mounted a narrow metal ladder, stood up on both clown feet and teetered unsteadily as he walked across a high wire, holding a parasol in one hand. As he balanced, he pretended to expel more gas. This brought uncontrolled hysteria from the male circusgoers. The well-dressed, Egyptian women to our right looked extremely uncomfortable but their children giggled and looked at their mothers, seeking permission to laugh.

More acts followed. A small parade of donkeys with feathers on their bridles trotted into the ring. Gymnasts jumped off and on their backs. We were beginning to wish we were back on the *Prince du Nil*, drinking wine, even Ptolemy wine, the brand name of a domestic wine sold in all first-class Egyptian hotels.

The tinny circus music blared out another Barnum and Bailey song. What we hoped would be the grand finale had arrived! A barred gate at the far side of the ring was raised and out leapt a tall man carrying a whip, splendidly attired in a top hat, spangled vest, and tights. He was accompanied by a woman wearing Islamic headdress and a pink, flowing gown, with billowing sleeves of transparent chiffon, held together at the wrist by sequinned birds. The man motioned two roustabouts, giving a signal to set up tall, metal barriers between the audience and the circus ring. The handlers wrestled the barriers into place, then locked them together, smiling to reassure the audience that it was now protected. The metal barriers secured, the lion tamer raised the barred gate. Within thirty seconds, out ambled a tawny lioness, her fur brushed and fluffed as if she had been given a blow dry at the local lioness coiffure parlor. She was followed by seven more big cats exactly like her. The softly padding circle of eight lions loped round and round the ring. After six turns, they leapt up onto big, trapezoidal stands. Here they sat, contentedly purring, looking no more ferocious than eight golden retrievers. They jumped through a series of hoops and bounded back again to their stands. Eight lionesses paraded gracefully and then leapfrogged over each other, never losing their poise or grace of movement.

Next, four lions lay down in a row on the ground, side by side in neat formation. The lion tamer's assistant, making a hand gesture signifying bravery, lay down next to the four butterscotch-colored beasts. Then, the other four lions lay down in a tidy row on her other side. She looked like pink icing in the middle of eight slices of oatmeal bread. The male audience groaned and gasped with approval and wonder at what they seemed to feel was the amazing sight of a fearless woman. The Egyptian women and children in their cordoned-off family section shrieked in terror. At last the lions were allowed to relinquish their supine poses and bound back silently to their stands. The woman stood up and raised her hands in a supplicating manner toward the audience, begging for approval and applause for her bravery. The lion tamer dismissed the big cats and they loped out of the circus ring and back into their cages. Somewhere behind the scenes we could still hear a few satisfying but muffled roars as the lions disappeared.

Applauding vigorously, we thought this was the end—but the show was not quite over. Out came two circus flunkies bearing an eight-foot wooden box. The lion tamer and his lady reappeared. One side of the box was raised and out of the long, thin coffin was lifted the tan-gray, muscular form of a giant python. The lion tamer put the middle section of the python around his neck and the python coiled tightly around him, giving him a gigantic, serpentine embrace with its massive, pulsating coils. The Egyptians gasped. Would the snake become carried away and, acting out its natural instincts, crush the lion tamer in a fatal squeeze? At first, the snake seemed to be increasing his deadly stranglehold. Then he began to loosen his grip and, wriggling a bit, straightened out and relaxed his coils. The woman in the pink dress patted the snake with her jewelled fingers; the serpent seemed to respond favorably to this act of friendship. Then, in a last gesture of supreme courage, the woman took the head of the python and inserted it into her mouth. The first evening performance of the traveling circus at Edfu had come to an end.

Overleaf: A peasant in Upper Egypt bids a sad farewell before selling his sheep at a local market. ▷▷

This woman sells cooking dishes on a Luxor street. She is prosperous by the standards of Egyptian town dwellers. When an Egyptian housewife has access to capital, she controls household supplies and may shift household tasks to her daughters-in-law. Thus, she may have more power than her husband or son.

◁ At Karnak a *ghaffir*, or custodian, stands in front of the colossal, standing statue of Ramses III outside his barque shrine in the first courtyard of the Temple. Looking through the doorway, there is an oblique view of figures of Ramses III in his Osiris form. The dark stain on the Temple wall running up to Ramses's elbow indicates the level to which the statue and the Temple were buried before excavation at the end of the nineteenth century.

Salt stains at the base of the statue show that ground water is still infiltrating the porous stone.

Overleaf: Sunset photographed from the top of the north wall of the Karnak Temple silhouettes the tip ▷▷ of the great obelisk of Thutmose I (1524–1518 B.C.), and the much taller obelisk of Queen Hatshepsut (1503–1493 B.C.). The hypostyle hall of the temple is to the right.

A felucca pilot on the Nile at Luxor. Some of these boatmen are adept at stranding tourists among the bulrushes of the west bank, then arranging for confederates to rescue them for handsome tips.

Egypt is an outdoor museum. A temple guardian seated before the statue of Tutankhamun, shown as Amun-Re, ▷ stands at Karnak Temple between the sixth pylon and the barque sanctuary of Philip Arrhideus (323–315 B.C.)

In the late afternoon, a *felucca* with its sails furled comes to rest at Kitchener's Island near Aswan. The design of these broad-beamed river boats, which carry passengers as well as produce, has not changed in two thousand years.

This characteristic headdress is used by Muslims as well as by some Oriental Christians and Jews. A knowledgeable observer can distinguish tribes and nationalities from the style of the turban and sometimes from the length of the cloth.

Near the Avenue of the Sphinxes, a Luxor peasant displays her prized possessions—two newly-born ▷ kids.

Overleaf: A villager in Upper Egypt dozes in the courtyard of his house. The inscription on the wall ▷▷ celebrates the *Hajj:* "The blessed pilgrimage has no reward except heaven."

حج بيت الحرام وزار قبر ...
... الحاج
١٩٨٥

بسم الله الرحمن الرحيم

قل هو الله أحد الله الصمد لم يلد ولم يولد
ولم يكن له كفواً أحد صدق الله العظيم

Egypt is famous for its superior donkeys. A wealthy Egyptian man may own a donkey with an elaborate stuffed saddle, the seat padded with soft, woolen lace. In the past, the animal was often preceded by a donkey boy who ran ahead to clear the way. Egyptian men who can afford to ride are rarely seen walking. Even today, women are usually seen on foot and in groups.

This *fellah*, or village peasant, is mounted on a pile of empty bags of imported wheat, part of the U.S. foreign aid program which allocates billions of dollars annually to Egypt.

◁ One of the guardians of the great hypostyle hall at Karnak Temple nonchalantly crosses an aisle. The columns in the central aisle have a girth of thirty-three feet and measure sixty-nine feet in height.

A guardian of the small Temple of Queen Hatshepsut (at Medinet Habu on the West Bank of the Nile across from Luxor), holds a crisp bunch of lettuce. On the relief behind him, probably recarved during the Ptolemaic Hellenistic period, is the fertility god, Amun-Min. Below his upraised elbow is a carving of endived-shaped "aphrodisiac lettuce."

A Luxor woman prepares greens for dinner. Her goat gets the leftovers. The contorted, cross-legged position is unusual for Egyptian peasant women, most of whom squat.

This is the house of a prosperous and devout Muslim who has completed the ▷ pilgrimage to Mecca. The wall painting on the right shows the *Haram*, or white marble courtyard, of the Holy Mosque at Mecca. The painting on the left depicts the *Ka'ba*, the sacred, cube-shaped, stone structure in the courtyard of this most sacred of mosques.

The inscription above the doorway in Luxor reads: "It is the duty upon people to make the pilgrimage to Mecca if people have the means to do so." This is the classic commandment for Muslims, not just the opinion of this Luxor householder.

Overleaf: The Tuesday buffalo market is fifteen miles from Luxor. After transporting ▷▷ their choice specimens from distant villages in the backs of Toyota trucks, wealthy stock breeders pass the day in trading, gossiping and smoking water pipes. At day's end, they leave with thick wads of twenty pound Egyptian notes.

The water buffalo is vital to the agricultural economy of Upper Egypt. Poor farmers are close to destitute if they lose their animals. The buffalos plough the fields and provide rich milk and cheese. Buffalo dung mixed with straw is also used to make cakes of fuel.

A Luxor woman sits by her intricately carved door. Most doors in Egyptian towns are azure which is the color of the Nile as well as the color that is thought to protect against the Evil Eye.

◁ These columns surround the courtyard of a small temple built by Ramses III (1184–1153 B.C.). Originally located in front of the Karnak Temple, the small temple was intended as a resting place for the sacred boat shrine in which the images of the god of Karnak, Amun, would rest before being carried out in procession by the priests. The colossal figure fronting the columns is the god Osiris.

◁◁ *Previous page:* The *fellahin*, or peasants, who live in this typical village in Upper Egypt are settled in their habits and virtues. Aside from the introduction of some diesel irrigation pumps and tractors, their primitive agricultural economy has changed little in six thousand years. In Cairo, some intellectuals say, ''look to the *fellahin*'' if you want to understand the true spirit of the pharaohs.

Overleaf: A brightly painted lintel over a passage connecting the second court of Medinet Habu Temple and the hypostyle hall ▷▷ retains much of the original color which has, unfortunately, faded away from most of the other walls in the Temple. The ceiling decoration features a winged sun disk. Behind, is an oval-shaped cartouche enclosing the name of Ramses III, the Temple's builder. Medinet Habu is on the west bank of the Nile, near the Valley of the Queens.

Even the poorest Egyptian housewife seeks out the spice sellers. These men have sacks of rose leaves, ginger, oregano, cinnamon, saffron, tumeric, marjoram and jars of cumin, sesame seed, cardamom, anise and hilba. Hilba is a seed sold to women who are lactating and who wish to increase their milk supply. A tealike brew is made from the seed.

195

While President Hosni Mubarak watches impassively from a wall poster, this town dweller from Upper Egypt enjoys a moment of smoking bliss.

◁ The venerable figure on the left resembles a religious patriarch, but, in fact, he is a prosperous merchant promoting his wares in Esna, a Nile river town.

◁◁ *Previous page:* Each spring, a traveling circus stops at the small river town of Edfu, south of Luxor on the Nile's West Bank. The sideshow tantalizes potential customers with promises of a snake woman endowed with a woman's head and a serpent's body. Also there are feats of levitation, a girl made of fire and electricity, and demonstrations of hypnotic trances. The grand finale is a woman of great courage who puts the head of a live python in her mouth! All of this in two shows a day.

199

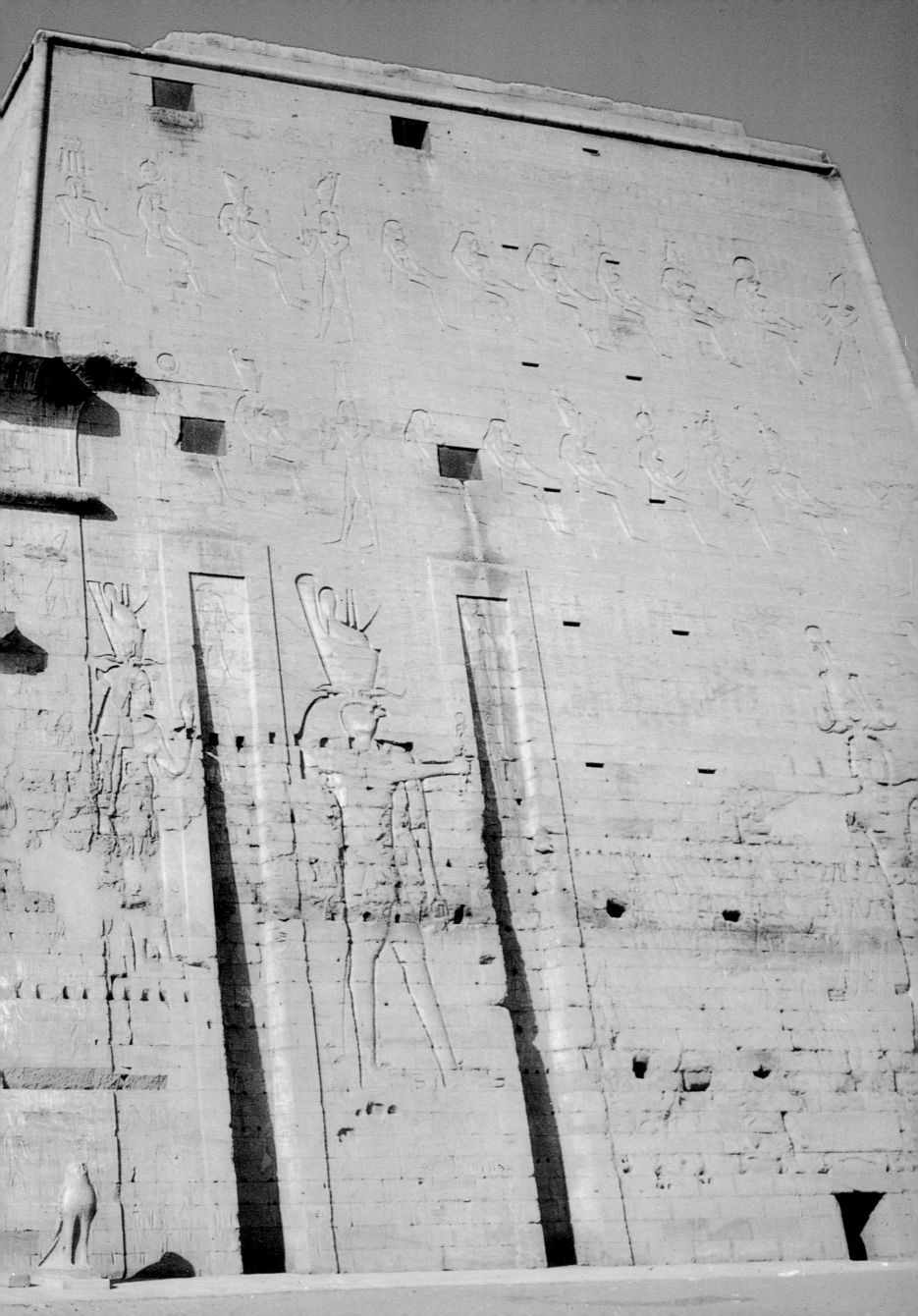

"The camel is a nasty, growling, grumpy beast. He is a contemplative, ruminative, speculative quadruped, more fitted for the desert than for the polite society of the animal world." —*Sir Arthur Silva White, 1899*

In the Corridor of the Bull at Abydos, two guards stand sentinel at the western exit. The corridor is part of the 3000-year-old ▷ Temple of Seti I. The temple reliefs are considered among the finest in Egyptian sculpture. The barrel-vaulted arch carved out of a single rectangular stone predates the Roman keystone arch by at least 1,000 years.

Abydos was once the holiest town in ancient Egypt. Home of the Osiris cult, Abydos was believed to be the place where the Goddess Isis brought the dismembered body of the God Osiris, assembled his remains, and brought him back to life.

◁◁ *Previous page:* Edfu is a market town sixty-five miles south of Luxor on the west bank of the Nile. The Sun God, Horus-Apollo, was particularly beloved and worshipped here. Horus was depicted in human form with a falcon's head or as the winged sun, as shown here under the cornice of the gateway.

Begun in 237 B.C., the Great Pylon of Edfu's Ptolemaic Temple is covered with beautifully preserved, carved reliefs of King Neos Dionysos delivering a powerful blow to his enemies. He is watched by the falcon-headed Horus and Hathor, the cow goddess. The two recesses on either side of the main entrance once contained flagstaffs.

Women in Aswan wait patiently for freshly baked loaves of bread. The Egyptian ▷
government may double the price of imported wheat, yet the subsidized price of a
loaf of bread often remains unchanged. This makes baking at home increasingly
costly.

◁◁◁ *The first of two previous page openings:* The checkerboard, red-and-white design used
on the external walls of this mosque in Abydos is common in Egyptian towns. The
crescent moon and star are traditional symbols of Islam. The use of the crescent did
not originate with the Arabs but with the Ottoman Turks who, in turn, adopted it
from the Byzantines after the conquest of Constantinople in 1453. A crescent on the
top cupola of a mosque indicates the direction of Mecca.

◁◁ *The second of two previous page openings:* In the barren desert west of Medinet Habu
near Luxor, the domes of Beir el Moharreb ("Monastery of the Warrior"), now the
home of a dwindling order of Coptic nuns, glisten in the sun. The large dome in the
foreground is the tomb of Dr. Labib Habachi, a beloved citizen of Luxor who died in
the early part of this century. In the fourth and fifth centuries, many of the desert
fathers in the early Christian church settled in both Egypt's Western and Eastern
deserts, living in complete isolation from the society of the Nile Valley. By the
Middle Ages, hundreds of Christian monasteries were flourishing in Egypt. In
modern times, their numbers have diminished drastically.

A worshipper, standing on the East Bank of the Nile, welcomes a new day, which, ▷ for followers of Islam, begins at sunset.

For Muslim believers, most days of the week are considered either auspicious or unfortunate. Sunday is maligned because the Prophet died on a Sunday night. Tuesday is called "the day of blood" because several famous martyrs were put to death on that day. On the other hand, Tuesday was once considered a day of choice for being bled for medical purposes. Wednesday is an indifferent or neutral day. Thursday is called *el mubarak*, or "The Blessed." Friday is holy above all other days of the week because it is the Muslim Sabbath.

◁◁ *Previous page:* A brother and sister enjoy themselves on a rudimentary swing in a free playground in Luxor's back streets.

Overleaf: Except for a few small shops, fishing is the only business in Shakshuk, a ▷▷ tiny village located on the shores of the Birket Qarun in the Fayoum. The inhabitants spend their days repairing the small fleet of fishing boats as well as tying and weaving nets.

These women live in Shakshuk, a tiny fishing village which stands on the edge of Qarun Lake in Fayoum Oasis. Most of the village families have intermarried and bear strong physical similarities. Qarun Lake was a favorite crocodile hunting ground for pharaohs in the Middle Kingdom.

As light winds fill his sail on a balmy, January day, this young fisherman in the ▷
Fayoum pulls in his lacy nets. He hopes for a bountiful catch of fish in the waters of
the Birket Qarun, a salt-water lake now unfit for drinking or irrigation. In pharaonic
times, the Birket was a huge freshwater resource for the people of the Fayoum.

◁◁ *Previous page:* Pigeon-raising is an important economic and dietary endeavor in
Egyptian villages. This double bird house in the Fayoum is made of clay pots inserted
in mud walls. Pigeons then lay their eggs in safety, the neck of the pots being too
small for large predators. The arrangement facilitates collection of the pigeon excre-
ment, which is used for fertilizer.

Journey
to
the Five Oases

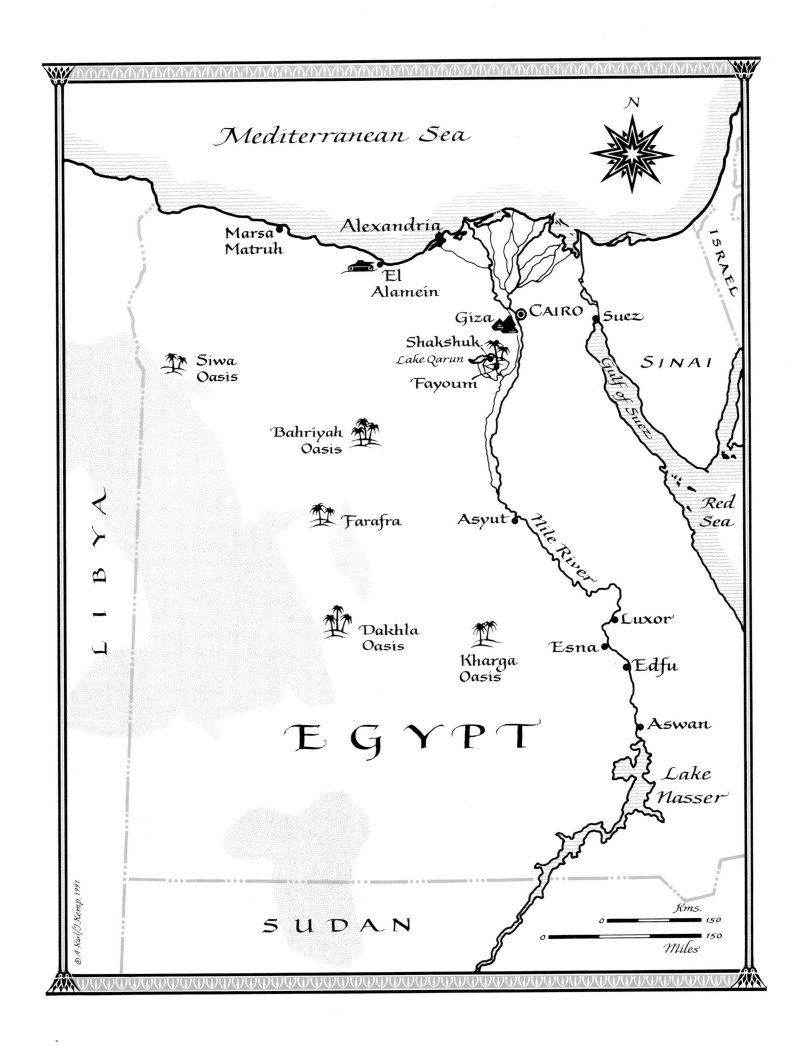

Mediterranean Sea

N

Marsa
Matruh

Alexandria

El
Alamein

Giza ○ CAIRO   Suez

Shakshuk

Lake Qarun

Fayoum

SINAI

Gulf of Suez

Siwa
Oasis

ISRAEL

Bahriyah
Oasis

Red
Sea

Farafra

Asyut

Nile River

LIBYA

Luxor

Dakhla
Oasis

Esna

Edfu

Kharga
Oasis

Aswan

EGYPT

Lake
Nasser

© A. Karl/J. Kemp 1991

SUDAN

Kms.
0   150

0   150
Miles

◁◁ *Previous page:* "A camel vaulted and huge-ribbed as an antique ship
. . . with a stride like an ostrich's. . . . a lyrical beast."
—*T. E. Lawrence (1926)*

Journey
to the Five Oases

To Siwa over the Sea of Stones

It was January. A few miles west of the Ras el Tin royal palace of the late King Farouk in Alexandria, on the road to Marsa Matruh, we suddenly entered a harsh and almost rainless desert. Seven of us were driving in a minivan along the shore of the Mediterranean Sea on a road dotted with Egyptian vacation resorts and signs in Arabic advertising Orange Crush. Soon we left the seacoast and headed west on a bone-rattling macadam road that traces the northernmost boundary of the great Libyan Desert. Egypt's portion of this vast expanse of sand and rock is known as the Western Desert, one of the most barren landscapes on the face of the earth. An area of 260,000 square miles encompassing two-thirds of Egypt, it is bounded by the Nile on the east and Libya on the west and stretches south from the Mediterranean coastline to the Sudanese border. Four hundred miles of uninterrupted sand lie between its Libyan boundary and the Pyramids of Giza. In parts of this desert, generations pass without a rain.

One hundred million years ago, all of Egypt was covered by ocean; today, shells and sea-life fossils are seen everywhere, embedded in stone or just lying on the sand. Throughout most of the Western Desert, there is only an inch or two of sand. Underneath is the glint of white or bare rock, bands of limestone and sandstone that reach down for several miles. Many geologists believe that below the Western Desert is a gigantic water reserve fed by rainfall from the mountains of the Western Sudan. If Egypt had ample capital and technology, she might realize here, in the Western Desert, Anwar Sadat's dream of a Green Revolution.

Less than fifty miles west of Alexandria, we detour to el-'Alamein, a mere spot in the desert where, in 1942, the great British victory reversed the German advance on Cairo and Suez. El-'Alamein is still littered with rusting tanks, unexploded land mines and miles of tangled barbed wire. The British cemetery commemorates the death of eight thousand British and Commonwealth soldiers. Each tombstone has a simple and heartbreaking inscription: "John Macleod, a wee laddie beloved by his Mum." In contrast, the German memorial, erected in 1959, commemorates the spirit of Nazi Germany. Like gunbarrels twisted in the heat of battle, the black, wrought iron gate that guards the entrance to the German tomb seems to depict the claws of carnage or the jaws of war. Like the rib cage of some monster or crippled, burnt-out panzer from Rommel's Afrika Korps, this gate leads to a giant hall known as the "castle of the dead," memorializing the common grave of four thousand German soldiers.

We were back on the main road west. The route to Marsa Matruh is the same desert track followed by Ramses II in 1250 B.C. and nine hundred years later, by the twenty-year-old Macedonian conqueror, Alexander the Great. The unrelenting, tan desert was broken here and there on the flat, coastal plain by rows of slate-green olive trees. Small, grayish shrubs marked the empty expanse of sand as far as twenty miles from the coast. These provided grazing food for flocks of black-headed Bedouin sheep which dotted the horizon, and were tended by Bedouin women and children dressed in bright, blue and green dresses. The Bedouin of the Western Desert, a tribe collectively known as the Alwad'Ali, have given up their tented life and are now housed in cement houses painted yellow, blue and pink and scattered in small settlements. Settled and agricultural, these desert folk grow olives and almonds and small crops of barley; they keep large herds of sheep for profit and small herds of camels for prestige. Bedouin who live near the desert highway are both dismayed and angered to see foreign travelers stopping to take photographs. They threw a few stones our way as we unthinkingly ventured into one of their small settlements. I did not realize that we were crossing a sacrosanct boundary line. Every Bedouin tent or house has an invisible, but inviolable, perimeter equal to the distance one can throw a stick.

As we approached Marsa Matruh, the sky suddenly disappeared and we were enveloped in swirling grains of sand. Sandstorms, particularly in an area of high dunes, can be fatal to travelers. Superstitions build around the terror of these storms. Some Bedouin believe that there are no sandstorms on moonlit nights or in the early evening, or before dawn. In truth, no time of day or night is safe. These fierce squalls usually last no more than five or six hours. They begin out of nowhere, coming suddenly in driving gusts. The entire surface of the desert seems to boil up as though a mysterious force was coming up from beneath the sand. Our storm continued to build. Pebbles struck my ankles. Swarming sand climbed my body and stung my face with blinding force. The world was blotted out. There were gusts, then lulls. We felt that we must keep moving, although the driving sand tempted me to stop and curl up. In such a storm, camels know instinctively that to stop is to be drowned in sand. Carburetors are stricken and spark plugs cease to function. We came upon dozens of Peugeots stranded on the roadside, hoods raised, their drivers desperate for aid. In olden times, these storms could destroy a caravan.

Today, Marsa Matruh, one hundred and fifty miles west of Alexandria, is a rather colorless town known mainly for its superbly protected port and dazzling white beaches. This ancient Egyptian resort, (marsa means harbor) the site of Queen Cleopatra's summer palace, flowered in Roman times with a large export trade of barley, sponges, dates and sheep. It was here in Marsa Matruh that Mark Antony, after the humiliating naval defeat at Actium by Caesar Augustus in 31 B.C., found love and consolation in the arms of his mistress, Cleopatra.

Night fell in Marsa Matruh and I was ready for bed. I took a final look at the city—it was winter: nothing but shuttered hotels and deserted beaches, small donkey-pulled, wooden carts with roofs and a flotilla of gray ships belonging to the Egyptian navy. The winds hurled huge, curling waves against the Mediterranean coast and chilled me to the bone. Cold seeped into the unheated hotel lobby, which was ornamented with dusty, plastic palms and green, naugahyde chairs.

The next morning we set off on the one-hundred-and-eighty-mile journey south from Marsa Matruh to the fabled Siwa Oasis. This trek used to be accomplished in six days on a fast-trotting camel or in ten days with a Bedouin caravan, lurching along a camel path only a foot wide, a rut worn over the centuries. Today, the journey can be made easily in three-and-a-half hours by motor on a first-class, military road. But now, there were delays due to the Egyptian military bureaucracy. The hassle of obtaining permits to go to Siwa from the police posts at Marsa Matruh added one day to the trip. The Egyptian-registered van driven by an Egyptian driver required an additional document. As Siwa is only thirty miles from the Libyan border, we needed a third stamped permit to enter a zone regarded as militarily sensitive. Egypt has maintained army units in desert areas near the Libyan frontier since the short Libyan war of 1977, but tensions have recently eased.

The military road is modern but the landscape through the Western Desert is parched and featureless. In early afternoon, distant sands turned into a shimmering lake. Far away, grazing camels were floating on a sheet of water. The water on the desert horizon gradually changed into rising waves of heat and then disappeared—a desert mirage. Other than this vision of "devil's water," there was very little relief to the endlessly rolling sand.

The monotony of the journey was interrupted by five lonely military checkpoints. At each one there was a handful of grim, khaki-clad soldiers wearing red berets and puttees, carrying rifles with bayonets fixed. Cursorily examining our travel documents and checking the likeness on each passport against our dusty, American faces, they waved us through the swinging gates of a barricade. At these stopping places there were no trucks or barracks, only red-and-white oil drums and a dilapidated tent or two, a wooden cage of chickens and an omnipresent can of precious, fresh water. As we drew closer to the Libyan border, numerous troop encampments and ominous gun emplacements appeared on hilltops. I wondered . . . how do these soldiers deal with the oppressive tedium of these desert outposts?

In Bob Hope movies, an oasis is a tiny spot in the desert with Dorothy Lamour lounging seductively under a solitary palm tree next to a tiny pond of fresh water. In romantic Victorian fiction, an oasis was a place inhabited by handsome sheikhs and their gossamer-clad paramours. In fact, the great oases of the Libyan flatlands, such as Siwa and Dakhla, are deep depressions in the arid desert capable of sustaining a settled community of up to sixty thousand people. For millions of years, driving springtime winds, the tail end of the monsoons that batter East Africa, have moved east, gathering speed and picking up sand as they travel hundreds of miles across the Libyan Desert. These powerful, abrasive forces work through weak points in the rocky desert surface and produce a classic, deep oasis such as Siwa.

The parched sands of the Libyan Desert gradually ascend to the high plateau of land ending in the cliffs that surround Siwa Oasis. Suddenly we left the high desert to begin our downward descent into the oasis seventy feet below sea level. Giant limestone cliffs towered on either side. Ahead, through myriad palm groves, was a shimmering stretch of salt lakes. We had entered the legendary oasis of Siwa, a magnificent green garden in the Libyan Desert, fifty-one miles long and seventeen miles wide, hidden in a sea of sand. The lakes were peacock blue and green. The setting sun flooded the scene, making evening in the oasis a glowing spectacle of pinks, purples and oranges.

The Siwans differ in appearance from the Egyptians and the Bedouin. They trace their ethnic roots to the Berber tribes who occupied North Africa from the Atlantic to Western Egypt in the eleventh century. Actually, they are now a mixed race, dating from medieval times when Siwa was the marketplace for slaves from the Sudan. Caravans bearing ostrich feathers, gold, ivory, leather and black slaves stopped in Siwa to exchange their treasures for succulent Siwan dates. Most Siwans have dark complexions but a startling few have straight hair, light skin and blue eyes. A majority of Siwans are competent in Arabic but they continue to speak a Berber language similar to that of the Tuaregs of Morocco. This particular dialect, used largely when they speak among themselves, is known to be spoken only in one other place, a village a few miles across the Libyan border. Today, there are still a few elderly Siwan men who know almost no Arabic, and many Siwan women (more isolated from outsiders than the men) who understand no Arabic at all.

In 1910, Dr. Douglas E. Derry of Harvard University studied one-hundred-and-eight skulls dating to Roman times which had been found in graves of the great Siwan necropolis. Measurements of crania, facial and nasal openings showed that Siwans were closely related to European stock. This insight ties in closely with the Siwans' Berber dialect and the surviving presence of those few light-skinned, blue-eyed inhabitants.[1]

Most historians believe that Siwa was colonized by Ramses III around 1175 B.C. Yet, no traces of the Old, Middle or New Kingdoms have been found in Siwa. By all accounts, Siwa was securely under Egyptian rule by 550 B.C. By then, it was renowned as the seat of the Oracle of Jupiter-Amun, which ranked with that of Delphi in prestige. The Oracle's seat was in the great temple of Amun, built in the sixth century B.C. on a large rock acropolis at the original Siwan capital of Aghurmi, which is four kilometers east of the present town.

Herodotus is the best source on ancient Siwa and its oracle. In Book III of his *Histories,* he writes of the Persian invasion of Egypt in 525 B.C., led by Cambyses, son of Cyrus. In Herodotus's words, Cambyses "detached a body of 50,000 men with orders to attack the Siwans, reduce them to slavery and burn the Siwan Oracle of Jupiter-Amun."[2] The Persian army departed from Thebes (the area near and around Luxor), and after seven days arrived one hundred miles west of the Nile at Kharga Oasis known to the Greeks as "Island of the Blessed." Herodotus tells us that the huge army disappeared somewhere in the desert midway between Kharga and Siwa, never reaching its destination.

Another story, related by the renowned Egyptian historian and archeologist, Ahmed Fakhry, holds that soon after the Persians left Kharga on their march across the desert, a wind of extreme violence drove the sand over them as they were taking their midday meal, whereupon they disappeared forever.[3] Thus Jupiter-Amun had his revenge on the would-be destroyers of his temple. Fakhry writes that while the size of the army was exaggerated, the historical fact remains that in 524 B.C., the army of Cambyses was buried midway between Kharga and Siwa. Almost 2,500 years later, in March 1984, a major sandstorm struck the Western Desert and uncovered a two-thousand-year-old Greco-Roman temple near Siwa. Several hundred graves were discovered containing bone fragments which archeologists believe may be the remains of the army of Cambyses.

Ultimately, Siwa fell to the Persians sometime around 500 B.C. Two hundred years later, in 333 B.C., Alexander the Great defeated Darius III, King of Persia, and liberated Egypt, including the Western Desert, from her Persian conquerors. Alexander's interest in Siwa was, in part, a natural outgrowth of his studies in Greece under his tutor, Aristotle. For hundreds of years before his defeat of the Persians, many temples of Jupiter-Amun had been built in Greek cities, modeled after Siwa's temple. Many philosophers came from Athens to study in Egypt, whose wisdom and mysticism were highly regarded by the Greeks. Alexander was also a passionate believer in the power of oracles; but other oracles had disappointed him in his quest to discover the mysterious origins of his ancestry. In 331 B.C., he interrupted his military campaign in the Western Desert to make a special visit to Siwa's oracle.

In Alexander's day, the trek from Paraetonium (now Marsa Matruh) was a long and perilous journey fraught with grave dangers of sandstorms and death from thirst and dehydration. According to the Greek chronicler Callisthenes, a contemporary of Aristotle, water ran out a few days into Alexander's march but the caravan was saved by a sudden and unusual rainfall. A few days later, a violent sandstorm blowing from the south obscured the desert track. Once again, the travelers were miraculously rescued, this time by two crows that led them with flapping wings and hoarse, raucous cries to Siwa's abundance. Grateful and eager to visit the Oracle, Alexander proceeded to the temple. According to this account, Alexander was received by the high priests of Amun and designated as "Son of Zeus-Amun, the master of all countries, unconquered till he is united with the gods."

Plutarch was less certain that the Oracle had assured Alexander of his divinity. According to this Greek historian, Alexander and his followers stood in the courtyard of the Temple where they gazed upon the golden statue of Amun decorated with emeralds, carved in the shape of a human navel, or umbilicus. The statue was placed on a barque and carried in a procession while female musicians dressed in flowing white robes sang and danced, accompanying the barque.[4] Alexander then entered the cella, or most holy place, unaccompanied. No one knows what questions the young king demanded of the Oracle of Siwa. No one knows if Alexander bribed the priests to win a favorable opinion, but he departed satisfied with the answers. From that day on, Alexander was a steadfast believer in Amun. Some records say that Alexander wanted to be buried in Siwa. But on his death at thirty-three in 323 B.C., he was encased in a gold coffin in Alexandria, the Egyptian city that he founded.

Although the northern and eastern walls are gone, much of the temple of Amun still stands and visitors may still see the courtyard, the remains of the damaged cella, and a well-preserved corridor that runs around the sanctuary. Historians believe that the high priests who articulated the wisdom of the Oracle secreted themselves in this corridor. The temple of Amun at Siwa functioned until the sixth century A.D., when it was closed by the Byzantine emperor, Justinian.

According to local history, the newer, medieval town of Siwa, founded in 1203 A.D., was a fortified bastion with a commanding view of the oasis. Its turrets, now in ruins, form a sharply jagged line silhouetted against the blue sky. The minaret of the fifteenth-century mosque is still in use. Siwa's original defense wall had only one gate. A century later, another entrance was cut, this time on the south. Known only to local inhabitants, the south gate could not be detected from the outside. Everyone was required to build inside the town walls and women were forbidden to leave the enclosed town. It was another hundred years before the town elders granted women permission to leave the village and enter the lush gardens. The streets of the medieval citadel were so narrow that two loaded donkeys could not pass. Sinuously twisting corridors made it easy to lose one's way. Even today, in the beehive-like old town, the labyrinthine passages still twist and turn as they pass under beams of date palm trunks covered with palm-frond matting packed with mud. The tumbledown structures and rubble of the oldest parts of Siwa now serve as pens for donkeys and goats.

As the population grew over the centuries, each family added as many as four additional floors to its mud house to accommodate newly married family members. The mud used as a building material was part gypsum, which, when dried, became as hard as concrete. Unfortunately, the mortar was vulnerable to rainstorms, infrequent as they are. Prolonged rainfall may come only once in a decade, but when rains do come, the salt in the mud dissolves and the town walls collapse.

After the protective occupation of Siwa by soldiers of Muhammed 'Ali in 1820, the Siwans began to feel secure from outside invasion. In 1826, the town council gave its first permission to build and live outside the original fortress walls. The old, honeycombed structures were difficult to ventilate and disease was rampant in the close, airless quarters. People were pleased when they were allowed to construct new dwellings at the foot of the old fortress where they had air and light, and in the new part of town no one was allowed to build to a height of more than two stories. A torrential, three-day rainstorm in 1926 resulted in massive destruction, leaving scores of sharply jagged battlements and devastated houses. In 1985, another major deluge caused more recently constructed buildings to collapse. Today, stone is being used, radically changing the quaint and organic appearance of the town.

In 1940, early in the North African campaign, the Italians bombed Commonwealth troops stationed in Siwa. The inhabitants fled for shelter to nearby Jebel el-Mawta (literally the "Mountain of the Dead"), the great necropolis one-and-a-half kilometers from Siwa town. They occupied ancient tombs, digging into the sides of the necropolis. They huddled together, jammed in with their chickens and goats. In the process, tombs, mummies, wall paintings and other artifacts dating back to the fourth century B.C. were uncovered.

In June 1942, Rommel's Afrika Korps was pressing eastward and the Allied troops withdrew from Siwa. A few weeks later, Italian forces marched into the oasis. Delighted to find spring-fed lakes and date-laden palms, they raised their flag over Siwa's police station. On September 21, Field Marshal Rommel visited Siwa and received an official welcome from the city fathers. He brought gifts of tea and coins to suspicious village elders who eventually invited him for tea in one of the oasis gardens. After Rommel's forces were defeated at el-'Alamein in the fall of 1942, peace returned to the oasis.

In Siwa today, as in the past, the traditional Arab female's fear of being seen or photographed is extreme. When married Siwan women leave their houses and cross from one street to another, they pull their blue-gray cloth *milayahs* around their heads and shoulders, leaving a small crack for eyes and nose, and hurry quickly around a corner or duck into a doorway. After puberty, young girls are not to be photographed at all. A young Siwan student says, "One hundred years from now, there are two things that it will be impossible to change—the Berber dialect and the *milayah.*" Such extreme modesty and fear of being seen by men worked to my advantage as an inquiring foreign woman. By leaving my male traveling companions behind, I greatly increased my opportunities to see, visit and photograph these reclusive women.

Like children everywhere, Siwan children have few of the fears of their elders. We were greeted by hordes of laughing children who stopped their frolicking and suspended for the moment their favorite activity of chasing the abundant, scurrying chicken population. Mothers send unmarried teenage daughters out to lure foreign women into their houses. I accepted one such invitation, and was able to see an immaculately clean dwelling almost devoid of furniture except for a single, wooden chest. Here, Siwan women hide their silver jewelry and embroidered wedding finery. Invariably, houses in Siwa look unfinished, as if waiting for another story to be placed on the open, standing walls. Principal household activities take place on the rooftops, where I discovered waterpots, clothes hanging up to dry, a few cooking utensils, cloth and straw mats for sitting or sleeping—and the inevitable chickens.

Inside Siwan houses, shyness gives way to potent, capitalist instincts, and Siwan women offer wedding dresses for sale, usually priced at about 100 pounds Egyptian ($45 American). Wedding, or "best" dresses, are sold in all five oases of the Western Desert. Precious, silver, virginity discs, symbolizing the purity of unmarried girls, are not for sale. But the women frequently sell their traditional modesty cloths, elaborately embroidered black silk shawls worn over the head and shoulders. The price of this stunning product, the result of four months of painstaking handwork, is usually 60 pounds Egyptian ($25 American).

For unmarried girls, synthetic fabrics imported from Taiwan (by way of Cairo), in gaudy, day-glow colors, now seem to be the fashion of the day. Shocking pinks and greens provide vivid spots of color in an otherwise uniformly mud-brown tableau. These garish, nontraditional imports will inevitably supplant the beautiful and time-honored native dresses.

Indeed, the pressures of the modern world were visible everywhere. Yet when I first caught sight of Siwa's conical mosques, her ruined medieval fortress, her tumbledown beehive houses, her circular springs of deep green water, her married women riding hunched over in donkey carts, entirely shrouded in blue-gray modesty cloths, and heard the strange cadence of the Berber dialect, I immediately knew that I had left the Nile Valley far behind and had entered a culture very different from either Cairo or Aswan.

Siwans refer to their oasis as the "paradise of the desert," and their golden crop is the palm date grown on two hundred thousand palms covering an area of thirty square miles. These savory dates, reputed to be the sweetest in the Middle East, are a staple of the Siwan diet. In the winter months, huge piles of orange dates lie drying in the sun at the side of every road and pathway. Each owner knows which pile is his, and an unwritten but sacred code guarantees the safety of each pile of dates. Since ancient times, traders have exchanged silks, mirrors, metal pots and mother-of-pearl for huge camel-loads of dates. According to tradition, the harvesters sang in praise of the bounteous date tree, and a Siwan fear was that shooting stars "hurled by angels in heaven at *jinn* (spirits) on the earth below would kill a date palm." Siwans today believe that if a traveler finds dates along his path, surely good fortune will follow throughout his journey. On the other hand, it was a cheering sight for a traveler to come upon the bleached bones of a camel skeleton shining white in the sand. This meant that a well was not far away: it was believed that camels are most likely to die at the end of a trek.

Olives, known in ancient times as "the gift of Athena," are the second crop in the oasis. The purple fruit is gathered and dumped into a primitive press. The screw is turned, and out comes a wine-colored oil which is salted and sold as a great delicacy throughout the Middle East. And in the lush oasis of Siwa, nobody goes to bed hungry.

With a population today of ten thousand people, Siwa boasts four tiny hotels, the best being a government guest house, simple but clean. I was assigned a room with toilet for $2.50 per night and electricity from 5:00 P.M. until midnight. I discovered that water was cut off in the bathrooms at 10:00 A.M. No meals were served, but a guest could take morning tea or coffee in the lobby. For our desert picnics, we bought tangerines and local bread in each oasis. The cheese, canned tuna fish and chicken were transported from home.

There is a local radio station at the oasis and television was introduced in 1986. I was told that over a thousand TV sets were sold in Siwa in one day—mostly on the installment plan. Siwan families gather around their sets in the evening, leaving the dark streets empty, as lights from the tubes flicker through windows. Siwans have become devotees of such American exports as *Falcon Crest.*

Siwa Oasis has only one hospital, but there are a plethora of mosques. Tucked into my bed, each morning, at the government rest house, I would awaken to a pleasing cacophony of donkeys braying, roosters crowing, and the sound of the *muezzins'* loudspeakers calling the faithful to prayer.

Marriage customs in Siwa are unique and elaborate. The night before her wedding, the bride goes to a sacred spring, accompanied by female members of her family. She is dressed in seven layers of silk, white next to the skin, followed outward by red, black, yellow, blue, red and finally green. Over these layers she wears an exquisite wedding dress elegantly embroidered in reds, greens, and yellows and decorated with hundreds of small, mother-of-pearl buttons. Most importantly, she wears the traditional virginity disc hung by a silver loop around her neck. Today, the solid silver of the past is alloyed with lead.

At the spring, the bride washes her face, hands and feet, and reluctantly removes the virginity disc, handing it to her mother, thus displaying both her sense of modesty and her sorrow at leaving home. The bride and her female relatives go forth from the spring, eventually meeting the women of the groom's family. Joining together in singing and dancing, they all process toward the bride's home. At last the bridegroom appears, flanked by male friends and kinsmen. The women of the two families engage in a mock fight which invariably results in victory for the bridegroom's kin, a relic of the tradition of marriage by conquest. The bride is driven to the groom's house by donkey cart or truck, accompanied by musicians playing cymbals and gongs. Her feet must never touch the ground. Reaching the groom's house, his kinswomen carry her into the bedchamber. The inviolate young woman wears a curved sword hung over her right shoulder. This scimitar is removed by the groom who carefully places it under the marriage bed to protect the couple from evil spirits. He presses her right toe with his right toe and feeds her fruits and sweets. Thus begins the wedding night.

Early the next morning, at call to prayer, the groom leaves the bride's bed. To avoid encountering his relatives, he hides away in the oasis gardens, where he remains until dark, creeping home to his new wife only after night has fallen. After the third day of this ritual, the couple begins a normal married life.

In the puritanical tradition of most of the Moslem world, Siwan women, before and after marriage, are cloistered and protected from any circumstance that might be sexually suggestive or titillating. Not even female donkeys are allowed in the town of Siwa; the carts are pulled exclusively by male donkeys. The reason, I was informed, is to avoid any chance incidents of animal copulation.[5]

I was surprised to learn that not all marriages in Siwa involve male and female partners. In the oasis, there is a class of unmarried, and often homosexual, males known as the *zaggalah.* Traditionally, these men work during the day as laborers in the oasis gardens of wealthy landowners. While these strong and able-bodied youths spend their days working, their leisure time is often devoted to singing and drinking *labgi,* a powerful local wine made from the heart of the date palm. They often perform erotic, homosexual dances, moving sensually in a circle with bodies touching. Until 1928, intricate legal marriage contracts were often drawn up between two *zaggalah* males. Celebrations of homosexual marriages were accompanied by large dowries, great pomp, and elaborate banquets. After 1928, King Fuad forbade marriage contracts between males, but until World War II, at least, the practice of homosexual marriage secretly continued without benefit of written contracts.[6]

In the oasis, segregation is a means of enforcing marriage expectations and controlling sexual behavior. Today, the *zaggalah* are obliged to live outside the limits of the town until they make traditional, heterosexual marriages. It is reported that until the early nineteenth century, widowers also had to live outside the oasis walls until they remarried.

In their isolation, Siwans have also developed a number of unique rituals and customs relating to birth and death that are not found in the rest of the oases or in the Nile Valley. The pre-World War II British chronicles on the Western Desert tend to be unabashedly colonialistic, producing probably inaccurate or exaggerated accounts of mores in the oasis. It may or may not be true, for example, that Siwan women resisted bearing children and used certain herbs and plants to prevent childbirth. One historian recounts that in the eighteenth century, newly-born females were thrown by their mothers off the high walls of the Siwan battlements.

Other customs in birth and death have been more reliably reported. It is only in Siwa, for example, that a mother lies on the bare floor for at least ten days after giving birth. After seven days of near solitude, she begins to hold court for female relatives and friends. The visitors enjoy a feast of edible clay, sweet cakes, and fruit. And, de rigueur on such occasions, is a very strong-smelling salted fish imported from Cairo which honors a revered Siwan saint.

If the new baby is a boy, the father chooses the name; if the child is a girl, the mother makes the decision. A midwife mixes a paste of henna and paints the cheeks of all the children of the household with an orangey-red stripe. The children run out of the house and into the street announcing the baby's newly chosen name, while the women remain in the house and place all their rings, bracelets and other silver jewelry in a large earthenware bowl.[7] The often toothless midwife recites the baby's name and the women ask Allah to avert all evil. Then the bowl is allowed to drop to the ground smashing into a thousand pieces. The awakened baby screams. Knowing that the demons and *jinn* have fled, the women collect their scattered jewelry and return to their homes.

In Siwa it is said, ''Death is the black camel that kneels at everyman's door.'' In accordance with Muslim practice, the dead are buried within twelve hours after death, and preferably before sundown. Piety requires the entire town to join in the mourning. As the women raise a piercing death wail, the body is carried by the mourners to the graveyard on a bier of olive wood, which is followed by a long procession of sheikhs, relatives, and townsfolk. The men chant a dirge and the women, swinging their veils, throw dust on their own heads. The body is buried on its right side, the face toward Mecca. The prayers remind the bereaved of the Prophet's words: ''The grave is the first stage in the journey to eternity.'' After the interment, family and friends return to the house for a funeral feast and for eulogies to the recently departed. Fakhry describes the custom of the *ghulah*,[8] or recently bereaved, outcast widow. When a male Siwan dies, his widow (who may be an old woman or a mere child of fifteen), follows the body to the burial ground. She then runs home. No one passes through the streets until she is out of sight. Dressed in white garments, the widow remains cloistered in her house for forty days without washing. She may not wear cosmetics or ornaments, or bathe. During this mourning period, only occupants of her house are permitted to see her. In past times, the period of seclusion, called *iddah* in Arabic, was one hundred days.

After her long confinement, the town crier runs through the streets announcing ''The *ghulah* is coming. Avert your eyes.'' The widow goes to a spring, washes herself, and now freed of all evil, she runs to her house and dons her finest clothes. The next day at dawn, she climbs to her rooftop and drops a palm stalk on the first person who passes in the street below. If it hits the target, a dreadful catastrophe will befall that passerby. Whether the stalk finds its mark or not, the widow is purged of all uncleanliness. A year must pass after her husband's death before she may remarry. Although the period of confinement of the widow is almost universal in the Arab world, the special tradition of the *ghulah* is unique to Siwa.

Kharga and Dakhla

We could have reached the Oasis of Kharga by a tedious one-hundred-and-twenty-five mile drive from the river town of Asyut, but on our second visit, we preferred a plane flight from Luxor. Through the centuries, Kharga was an important stop in the pilgrimage route connecting North Africa and Mecca. In the Western Desert, camel caravans moving east stopped first at Siwa, went then to Bahriyah, Farafra, and Dakhla and finally to Kharga.

Descending a thousand feet or more into a giant depression in the desert, we came to Kharga City, a charmless town of forty thousand people. The streets are wide, modern and without distinction. There may be no quaint streets or ancient doorways, but there are several simple and comfortable hotels, many modern houses and schools, clinics and government buildings. Most inhabitants of modern Kharga are recent immigrants from the Nile Valley.

In old Kharga, I explored the hidden, last vestiges of a medieval city of dark labyrinths and twisted passages, similar to those of old Siwa but even darker. Impoverished Kharga citizens still inhabit some of these honeycombed dwellings. C.A. Hoskins, a British traveler to Kharga in 1837, comments on the pale countenances of the women, their earrings of gold, rings in their noses and dresses decorated with shells. In a village homogenized by immigration from Cairo and the Nile Valley, gold nose pendants and traditional chin tattoos have vanished.

Prior to World War II, Kharga was used by the government as a quasi-penal colony for upper-class offenders. An army officer or government bureaucrat charged with crime or corruption had the choice of dismissal from government service or banishment to either Kharga or Dakhla Oasis. As a result, the opportunities for corruption moved from the Nile Valley to government reclamation efforts in the desert.

In the 1960's, the Egyptian government instituted population resettlement in the Kharga area of the Western Desert. In hopes of absorbing some of the exploding Nile Valley population, the government instituted a grandiose New Valley plan which called for drilling deep wells, thereby launching major agricultural projects in the sandy, desert soil. Kharga City was selected as the capital of the project despite the fact that it is chronically threatened by giant sand dunes that advance glacially and eventually smother Kharga's fields, date palm groves, and houses. South of the city, many new villages have been established, landless farmers from Upper Egypt resettled, and thousands of acres of new land brought under cultivation. But salinity problems have developed and the project is not yet self-supporting. The development plan staggers ahead, still a huge gamble for desperately impoverished and overpopulated Egypt.

On the outskirts of Kharga City lies a spectacular Christian necropolis, el-Bagawat, a huge, mud-brick, burial ground composed of hundreds of elegant, domed tombs, many still ornamented with biblical illustrations and Roman inscriptions. Archeologists have discovered the written correspondence of a society of grave diggers and embalmers who lived in Kharga at the end of the third century A.D. While it is impossible to date any tomb specifically, these graceful structures were built between the second and seventh centuries, and were originally used by pagans and Christians alike. El-Bagawat ceased to be a Christian burial ground in the seventh century, when the Arabs overran Egypt. With the spread of Islam, Kharga continued to be an important stop for those making the *Hajj* to Mecca. Graffiti scratched by thousands of pilgrims are still in evidence on the walls inside el-Bagawat's tombs.

In most parts of the world, nature has no sympathy for the archeologist, since it usually buries ancient cities in deep layers of dirt. But in Dakhla Oasis, nature is on the side of the scholar. Over the years, the eroding force of Sahara winds has exposed a rich collection of ancient artifacts. A team from Toronto's

Royal Ontario Museum recently discovered a mother lode of archeological treasures including flint hand axes and scrapers dating from the Old Stone Age (250,000 to 10,000 years ago). From the New Stone Age (beginning in 7800 B.C.) the Canadian archeologists have unearthed primitive agricultural tools and rock art drawings, relics of the period when stone age hunters of the Sahara first began to develop agriculture and animal husbandry. The remains of Persian water wheels, Roman stone temples, Byzantine frescoes and ancient mud-brick farm houses have been discovered as well.

The spread of Islam across North Africa in the seventh century produced a cultural and economic renaissance in Dakhla. The oasis became the Egyptian port of entry for a lucrative trans-Sahara trade in slaves, gold and ivory. All vestiges of the ancient trade have totally vanished. Today, mundane agriculture is the foundation of Dakhla's oasis economy; its dates, oranges, and tangerines are sold at bargain prices on every street corner.

We reached Dakhla on a macadam road that stretches one hundred and twenty miles from Kharga, passing giant sand dunes and miles of telephone poles half buried in slow-moving sands. On the eastern edge of the oasis is the tiny village of Bashendi. A pastel, picture book town of painted mud houses and soft curved walls, its architecture seems organically connected to the soil. On the town's edge, near the largest mosque, are two houses constructed of mud brick and creatively joined by a sunny, walled courtyard. Unlike any other houses in Bashendi, doors and windows opening onto this court are framed by ancient Egyptian design motifs painted in cheerful turquoise and white on the mud walls. This complex is the dig house of the Royal Ontario Museum's team of archeologists, medical doctors, and artists. Each December, scholars come to Bashendi from all over the world to live and work for three months, excavating, documenting, and studying the most ancient archeological sites in the Western Desert. In the courtyard, I saw leather buckets stuffed full of human bones and skulls, shards of ancient pottery, water jars thousands of years old, all carefully tagged, catalogued and painstakingly pieced together.

The Bashendi dig house was our home for four days. My room was a tiny, mud-walled, inside enclosure, the only daytime illumination coming from an eighteen-inch hole in the ceiling. At 6:00 P.M. each evening, we were grateful for Dakhla's newest amenity—electricity delivered to a feeble bulb hanging from the ceiling. When the moon rose, a bit of white luminescence made its way onto my sleeping bag.

In exchange for the gracious hospitality of the archeologists and the well-cooked evening meals of local chickens and oasis vegetables, we presented our hosts with a large bottle of Scotch whiskey which was consumed in twenty-four hours. Like the liquor, our tins of Plumrose potted ham were a forbidden treat in Muslim lands. We also came up with a few Hershey bars, and the diversion of news from the outside world.

The Toronto scholars are studying both the biological characteristics and the causes of death of the ancient Dakhlans. Skeletons from 1600 B.C. show that life expectancy at that time was only twenty-three years, 26 percent of the populace dying by age six and, surprisingly, 10 percent living beyond sixty years. In 1982, Professor Anthony Mills, the distinguished and genial head of the Dakhla project, uncovered a stone temple some thirty-five meters long, buried up to its roof in a sand dune. Subsequent excavations revealed high-quality relief carvings, suggesting that Augustus Caesar (27 B.C.–14 A.D.) was involved in the construction of the temple.

Perhaps the most thrilling of recent archeological discoveries at Dakhla was the unearthing of two rare, wooden books whose pages are literally a stack of paper-thin boards. One volume contains an essay on kingship by Isocrates, a fourth century B.C. contemporary of Aristotle. A second wooden book, found at the same site, provides crop ledgers written seventeen hundred years ago by the local agent of a distant landlord. It is a remarkable and authoritative account of the life of a Dakhlan who lived three centuries after the birth of Christ.[9]

Waiting for the sun to rise above the cliffs which surround the oasis, I ventured each morning into the streets, camera in hand. Soon after dawn, women carry water into their houses from the town pumps, sweep the dirt streets, dress the children and prepare breakfast on the open rooftops. The men drive their rickety, donkey-pulled carts to the fields. At 8:00 A.M., children troop off to the government-run elementary school. During the day, Bashendi town becomes a community of women, sitting on doorsteps weaving baskets, sieving grain in huge hoops, and washing clothes in giant aluminum pans, or *tishts*. Dakhlan baskets are usually woven of cream-colored palm and ornamented with red, blue, or purple designs. They are less finely made than Siwan baskets and far less expensive. All Bashendi women wear silver bracelets which they can often be persuaded to sell to foreigners. As in Siwa, they will part gladly with their best dresses for forty U.S. dollars. Local silversmiths are a dying breed; the bracelets come from Alexandria.

In common with rural Arab women almost everywhere, the Bashendi women are shy and are dismayed at the sight of a photographer's lens. With an almost intuitive sense that a camera was present, they ran away at my approach, laughing among themselves. Apparently there is no superstition that the photographer is stealing their souls nor do the Bashendi cover their faces with a cloth as women do in many parts of Egypt. It seemed that outwitting the camera was more of a game than a rigid cultural obligation.

Crossing the White Desert: Farafra to Bahriyah

Known by desert travelers as "the land of the cow," as some Egyptologists believe, in honor of the ancient Egyptian cow goddess Hathor, Farafra is the smallest of the major oases of the Western Desert. Lying halfway between Bahriyah and Dakhla, Farafra was once blessed with eighteen fresh water springs. Water sources at Farafra have now dwindled to ten, supporting a population of less than fifteen hundred people. We reached Farafra by automobile from Dakhla, traveling north along a difficult, bumpy road, one-hundred-and-ninety-miles long, in many places, entirely buried in sand.

According to the archeologist Fakhry, the people of Farafra have both Arab and Libyan blood. The European or Berber strain was immediately apparent; Farafrans are distinctly lighter-skinned than their neighbors in Dakhla or Bahriyah. But the culture seems homogeneous. Farafra is a timeless and unhurried community, where, prior to 1970, mail came once a month and few citizens had watches. The crude sundials still used in Farafra are in stark contrast to the natives' reputation for a vast knowledge of astronomy. Each citizen is well versed in the constellations and most Farafrans can tell from a glance at the stars how many hours remain until dawn.

The telephone system in Farafra rarely works and there is little trade or communication with the outside world. The townspeople raise sheep, cultivate dates, apricots and olives and there are small groves of orange and lemon trees. Farafran men have developed a small cottage industry of handknitting. With needles flying, they sit gossiping in the streets, making sweaters, vests and hats from the silky, cream-colored wool of local sheep.

I encountered one young man who showed unusual entrepreneurial hustle. In his mid-twenties and Farafra born, he dressed in western style and was the owner of an enormous, shiny, Japanese motorcycle. He had attended an art school in Cairo and had recently opened a small "museum" where he sold his own folk paintings. The gallery was also decorated with a few small stuffed gazelles (one of the few large animals remaining in the Western Desert), and some examples of crude, wooden locks still used to secure valuables in many Farafran houses. His paintings depicted daily life in the oasis including renderings of local knitters and old men playing an Egyptian version of checkers, using black and white stones. Few tourists come his way, but his salon in the oasis is a lively spot and some of his paintings have a pleasing, primitive quality.

Contrary to popular belief, the Sahara, of which the Libyan and Western Deserts are a part, is not an uninterrupted expanse of trackless waste. Between Kharga and Dakhla, for example, huge sandstone rock formations as much as forty or fifty feet high, rise out of a gently rolling desert. Over the centuries, the rocks have been eroded by mighty sandstorms. Half close your eyes and squint. You will see that the eroded rocks resemble huge camels, crudely carved sphinxes, and pyramids. On the same road, I saw that the rocks bear brilliantly colored iron striations of red, yellow, ochre, and purple. Pigments mixed from these deposits are used by local artists in Bashendi to ornament the walls of houses with beautifully colored *Hajj* paintings. The same mauves and ochres are used to illustrate biblical stories on walls inside the tombs of el-Bagawat, the Christian necropolis at Kharga.

Between Farafra and Bahriyah, the land is familiarly called "the white desert." We passed through a wonderfully mysterious area of strange, chalk-white and lumpy rock formations. Numbered in the thousands, these outcroppings are strangely rounded and are somewhat taller than an adult male—a surreal land of white Mongolian yurts or Alaskan igloos. I could not help thinking of giant, melting, vanilla ice cream cones.

Our drive through "the white desert" was jolting and slow. Groaning in anticipation, Samir Abu Bakr el Said, our driver, feared we might break an axle on the deeply-grooved roadway. Stones flew up from the roadbed like a spray of missiles, as, after dark, we bounced our way into Bawiti, capital of Bahriyah Oasis. Our destination was the Alpenblick Hotel, heralded in the guide books under "How to Do Egypt on Five Dollars a Day." Until recently, the Alpenblick had been owned by a Swiss hotelier who lived in Bahriyah for twenty years, playing host to a small but regular stream of European backpackers out from Cairo to "see an oasis." With high sandstone cliffs surrounding the oasis, the area is affectionately called "the Egyptian Alps," and it reminded the innkeeper of home. Hence the hotel's bizarre name.

Bahriyah is the easiest of the five oases to reach from Cairo. A public bus goes round trip once a day. We were advised that our rooms were priced at $1.25 per night. After a cursory inspection, one of us grumbled that perhaps they were overpriced. Our in-house philosopher and traveling companion commented acerbically, "This is no better than a caravansery." Each stuffy, windowless chamber was furnished with a mud-brick *mastaba*, or slab, for a bed, covered with a tired and dirty spread, a mud-brick table, a twig ceiling, and on the floor, a small pile of Kleenex, human hair, and cigarette butts—artifacts left by earlier occupants. Each room had one light bulb swinging nakedly from the ceiling, suspended by a dangerously frayed wire. There were no locks on the doors. In the course of my first fifteen minutes in the room, five different turbaned heads opened the door and looked in. As a sixth head with a leering smile, or so I thought, poked its way into my room, I decided to take my sleeping bag and move to a spare *mastaba* in my friends' room down the hall.

The location of the Alpenblick's highly-touted bathrooms was indicated by the folk art drawing of a toilet inserted between the "toi" and the "let." The bathrooms came complete with sinks without faucets and no suggestion of pipes underneath. The western toilets, pride of the Alpenblick and probably the only ones in Bawiti, were unconnected to any kind of plumbing.

Members of the Dakhla archeological team spiced up the conversation over our evening meal with hair-raising accounts of travelers who had decided to forego the dubious comforts of oasis hostelries and had chosen instead to sleep under the desert stars. One such camper, we were told, lost her life, ripped to pieces by a pack of ravenous hyenas. All things considered, perhaps the Alpenblick wasn't really so bad.

Bahriyah Oasis is eleven miles long, five-and-a-half miles across and contains a mixed ethnic population of 6,000 people. The excavations here have produced the remains of a Ptolemaic stone temple honoring Alexander the Great, a rare Egyptian burial tomb containing mummified birds, the remains of a Temple of Amasis decorated with important bas reliefs, and catacombs of Isis from the twenty-sixth Egyptian dynasty.

Writing in the 1930s, Fakhry noted that Bahriyahan women were more beautiful than those of Siwa or Kharga, adding also that women in Bahriyah are more free to join men in social gatherings of tea drinking. These women are famous for their lyrical "millstone songs," lines of poetry recited to the groaning rhythm of the stone mills used to grind the local grain.[10] Until recently, young Bahriyahan girls and their mothers, on leaving their homes, wore dresses of black cloth, richly embroidered in red, green and yellow silk and decorated with small metal coins made of genuine silver if the family was wealthy. The women of Bahriyah still offer these dresses to travelers, reluctantly parting with them for the equivalent of forty American dollars.

As in Siwa, Bahriyahan wedding customs are anomalous and loaded with Bedouin machismo. Fakhry recounts that, in preparation for the marriage ceremony, a bride is dyed with henna on hands, legs and feet. She is then brutally deflowered by her bridegroom, while three women hold her down. Then the bridegroom and his entourage fire their rifles into the air and the groom proudly displays the bloodstained undergarment to an expectant crowd of relatives waiting to make sure that once more the family honor has remained inviolate.[11]

At death, Bahriyahans place a waterpot on the burial place of the deceased and fill it each Thursday when the women of the family visit the grave bringing cakes and fruit to the tomb. Funerals at Bahriyah are accompanied by piercing screams, hysteria, and breast beating. Even the men participate in unrestrained weeping. The Bahriyahans believe that the soul of the deceased may return to the tomb in the form of a bird.

There are other forms of burial in the desert, often unplanned. The next morning we left the Alpenblick and set out once more on the monotonous, long road to Cairo. Suddenly, we came upon a grisly apparition: the seared carcasses of three camels, each upside down and half buried in the sand, twelve bleached leg bones sticking straight up. The desert is always the victor.

A doorway still standing on the heights of the medieval town of Siwa frames a view of crumbling fortifications and a modern minaret. Much of the medieval heart of Old Siwa has been abandoned, either because of termites chewing at the palm log beams or because the salt-saturated mud bricks have actually melted in the infrequent rains which can come centuries apart. Once a collapse occurs, Siwans often find it cheaper and easier to build elsewhere rather than to try to repair their old homes.

As late as the 1920s, the British traveler, Dalrymple Belgrave, wrote of Siwa:

''a group of witches live among some ruined houses in the highest part of the old town. Their leader is a blind woman who is said to be 100 years old. . . . She creeps about, leaning on a staff, like a regular witch in Grimm's Fairy Tales, and although she is quite blind, she manages to slip about the high battlements like a lizard, knowing by habit every stone in the place.''

In the dusky evening, the town still gives off a mood of mystery and hidden secrets, including superstitions and a fear of strange spirits—jinn, 'afrits.

In Siwa Oasis, thirty-three hair braids, each with three strands, represent the ninety-nine names of Allah. This Siwan girl has covered her hands in henna, which is considered a healing powder, even for the sore pads of the camel's feet. Hands and feet are also dyed with henna for marriages, circumcisions, and other important celebrations. Bedouin women who are turning gray but who wish to look youthful often use henna to dye their hair bright orange.

Siwan brides' dresses are always black or white with exotic sunburst designs and are shaped like a huge ''T.'' This bride wears black silk embroidered and laden with geometric designs of mother-of-pearl buttons. Both the silk embroidery and the tassles of her black modesty cloth represent the colors of dates in their various stages of ripening. This woman also wears a number of elaborately engraved silver heirlooms. (Some brides may wear as much as twenty pounds of silver at one time.) Her heavy earrings are fastened to a cloth band and hang from the top of her head, covering her ears. Called a *tilaqayn,* this arrangement includes heavy silver chains ending in pleasantly jingling bells attached to crescent-shaped disks. Siwan women never wear veils.

Two young Siwan boys display a *margunah,* a conical basket woven from fibers of the finest date palm leaves. Girls about to be married weave these baskets as part of their dowries. They are ornamented with silk, leather, and mother-of-pearl buttons. Considered to be the finest in all Egypt, the baskets are so closely and delicately woven that they will hold water.

Due to their Berber ancestry, some people in the Siwa Oasis have blue eyes and blond hair. But this teenage girl is part Nubian. After the sixteenth century, Nubians were brought to Egypt as slaves.

Overleaf: Camels prefer to follow rather than lead. The head camel in a caravan must be driven with a stick. ▷▷ They groan, growl and constantly complain while being loaded. The camels pictured here cross the "Sea of Stones" in Egypt's Western Desert, its rocky terrain covered with a thin layer of sand. The camel is the most precious possession of the Bedouin. "He who does not risk his life for his camel does not deserve to own him," goes a Bedouin saying.

A Siwan man stands beside his children in the main living room of his house. Siwan houses are almost bare of furniture. The ladder leads to the roof where food is prepared and where Siwans sleep on hot nights. The baby has a hat with a ruffle on the top, resembling the dorsal fin of a dinosaur. This style of bonnet seems unique to Siwa.

Elaborately-carved lintels decorate buildings in the medieval town of el Qasr—Dakhla Oasis. ▷

Overleaf: When Napoleon first saw the great Pyramids, he said to his generals: "Forty centuries look down upon ▷▷ you." The Pyramid of Cheops, in the middle, is 450 feet high, covers thirteen acres, and is constructed of two million limestone blocks.
Oblivious to the nearby grandeur, this camel anticipates a meal of clover after he has carried a few more loads of tourists around the pyramids.

A Siwan teenager drives his mother in the family *karussah,* a long donkey-drawn cart. Only a man or a boy is permitted to drive the cart. No male donkeys are permitted in the town. The conservative Siwan men do not want their women to be reminded of sex in any form. This woman is on her way to a fresh-water spring where she will socialize with other women while doing the family laundry. Except for this weekly chore, women leave their houses only to visit a relative or to attend weddings, circumcisions, or special feast-day celebrations. The Siwan men are responsible for going to market.

On the streets, a married Siwan woman always wraps herself in a *milayah,* shown here. The *milayah* in Siwa is a wide sheet of blue cloth woven in the village of Kirdassah which is near the Giza pyramids, on the caravan route to Siwa. When a woman sees a stranger, she pulls the *milayah* over her face, leaving a tiny hole for her eyes. If she encounters a stranger on the street, she quickly scurries into the safety of a neighboring doorway.

Married women of the Bedouin Awlad 'Ali tribe in the Western Desert are distinguished by brightly colored, full- ▷ length dresses, red cummerbunds and wide, silver bracelets. The red belt symbolizes femininity and fertility. It is considered indecent among the Awlad 'Ali tribe for married women to go without it.

◁◁ *Previous page:* The medieval town of Siwa was founded in 1203 A.D. The fortifications command a stunning view of the lush gardens of the oasis. On the left, is the simple minaret of the thirteenth-century mosque which is still used for prayers.

This severely retarded boy lives in the tiny Bedouin village of el-Khartoum. Everyone in the village treats him with great tenderness and affection. The insane, the slow and the mentally disabled are not outcasts in Bedouin society. But their handicaps prevent them from developing the Bedouin ideals of self-control, self-mastery and physical stoicism. Accordingly, they are said to be "without honor."

◁ This man is chief of the Bedouin settlement in el-Khartoum, a village south of the Kharga Oasis. Owning a herd of thirty camels, he is the most prosperous man in the settlement.

◁◁ *Previous page:* Bedouin women and children from el-Khartoum village near Kharga Oasis dress in brightly colored dresses. The two young women in the back are undoubtedly style setters in the village. The bobby pins and the yellow pom-poms of cotton worn on the head are considered chic and somewhat avant garde.

Baby boys are considered prey for evil spirits, so this young mother in el-Khartoum, a Bedouin village situated in the desert near Kharga Oasis, will dress her son in nondescript clothing until he has reached the age of two. Some mothers actually dress their tiny sons in girls' clothing and pay the midwife not to disclose the infant's sex.

This Bedouin girl lives in el-Khartoum, a small settlement in the Western Desert. She wears a home-sewn dress made from ▷ cheap, government-subsidized, flannel cloth bought on ration cards. Her perfect, white teeth are amazing, considering the fact that she has never owned a toothbrush.

An inquisitive man peers from the window of his house in Kharga, the great oasis southwest of Luxor. His window shutters have been painted blue as a safeguard against malevolent spirits.

◁ Children with masks stand on a street corner in Kharga Oasis. Running suits have become popular even in remote areas. The fashion began when Egyptian workers returned from jobs in Saudi Arabia and other oil-rich countries where they were exposed to western styles.

The older brother in this Bahriyan family of three girls assumes a sultan-like pose. The following Tunisian lullaby reflects the prevailing attitude toward female children throughout the oases.

"She who gives birth to a girl
Deserves to be hit with a pottery mug
And her husband not to sleep with her anymore.
She deserves his anger.
She deserves to be tied up and hung from a vine tree.

"But she who gives birth to a boy
Deserves the minaret and the village,
Deserves a basket of henna,
Jingling anklets,
A sheep slaughtered for her,
Great celebration, a big barbecue,
And the fat tail of a sheep."

◁ In Bashendi, Dakhla Oasis, stands the house of *Hajji* Mansur and *Hajjia* Fatima who recently accomplished the *Hajj,* or pilgrimage to Mecca. The wall inscriptions read: "Goodness upon those who know the *Qur'an.*" "There is no questioning the pilgrimage and what goodness it creates. God alone knows."

◁◁ *Previous page:* The Christian cemetery, el-Bagawat near Kharga Oasis, was begun in the mid-second century A.D. and abandoned about the seventh century. Wealthy people were buried in the chapels, poor people in the pits between the chapels. The hundreds of domed, mud-brick tombs follow the Coptic style; tomb facades are decorated with pilasters and half columns. The large apses of the more elaborate tombs resemble basilicas.

A few monuments are decorated with paintings showing stories from both the New and the Old Testaments. The colors used are ochre, mauve purple and grapejuice red, all made from earth pigments found in desert rocks.

Kharga Oasis was an important stop on the pilgrimage route between North Africa and Mecca. Early graffiti were left inside the chapels by thousands of pilgrims and other Arabs traveling by caravan.

On a wall in Farafra Oasis is a remarkably ambitious *Hajj* painting, with stenciled borders and a painstakingly depicted crowd of worshippers in Mecca surrounding the *Kaʿba*, the most sacred shrine of Islam.

◁ A Bashendi housewife prepares to lock up her goats for the night in an annex attached to her house.

A crippled man in Bashendi, Dakhla Oasis is unable to work. He is financially supported by his unmarried daughter who still lives at home.

In the deserts and villages of the Middle East, the bones of animals are believed to have magical ▷ powers. To ward off the ever-present Evil Eye, the skull of a gazelle or a donkey is hung by the gate. To ensure a bountiful date harvest, an animal bone may be hung in the branches of a date palm.

Overleaf: The area in the Western Desert between Bahriyah and Farafra Oases is called the White ▷▷ Desert. Here are thousands of bizarre, white limestone mounds resembling Mongolian yurts or melting ice cream cones.

In the hot, desert sun, Farafra, the smallest of the five major oases, presents a prosperous facade. The walls of the houses are covered with paintings of shrines in Mecca. Compared with the inhabitants of the four other oases of the Western Desert, the citizens seem less shy and more hospitable to visitors and enjoy showing off their houses and gardens. Visitors are invited inside for a glass of strong mint tea.

This woman holds a wooden key of ancient design. Around her neck is a modern key which opens a wooden box in which she keeps a few treasures: amulets and jewelry. Oasis women almost always own such a box.

◁ Village dwellers in Bashendi have a fine sense of beauty and design. The interiors of their houses are stark in their simplicity. An earthenware water jug may sit in a corner, perhaps the sole object in the room. Exterior walls are embellished with saw-tooth patterns, but this decoration, too, is used sparingly. Even everyday dresses exhibit a flair for color and elegance.

273

A girl in Dakhla Oasis raises her eyes from a tattered *Qur'an*.

A goat maintains a vigil at Bashendi in Dakhla Oasis. The ▷
mud-brick houses have triangular openings for ventilation.

In Bashendi village, Dakhla Oasis, two pieces of palm ribs are placed on a man's grave. Villagers believe that when an old person dies, a younger person will soon die, also. To prevent this grim occurrence, all the stones left over from building the tomb are removed. The unavailability of building materials assures continued life. The wooden bier used to carry the body to the grave is placed upside down on the tomb and covered with stones.

This mother and child live in Bashendi, a small village in Dakhla Oasis. In Egyptian villages one never says, "what a ▷ lovely baby." Instead, the mother prefers to hear, "what a hideous little creature" or "what an ugly monster." Even repugnant names may be given to children to protect them from the Evil Eye. Anwar Sadat's widow, Jehan Sadat, tells the story of a child who was named "beggar" by his mother. With such a name, no one would believe the child to be sound and healthy and the little one would have a better chance of surviving to adulthood.

Overleaf: There seem to be no right angles in the village of Bashendi, Dakhla Oasis. The architecture appears to have an ▷▷ organic connection with the soil. Small triangles in the wall provide a repeated design motif as well as minimal ventilation and light. The streets are swept each day and goats help keep them free of trash.

El sega.TheoLdesT.game.For.oLd.peopLe.infarafra.

In the oasis of Farafra, a young artist offers a painting for sale. His work depicts local men engaged in knitting sweaters, vests, socks and hats. Also shown is the popular Egyptian game of Sega, played on twenty-five squares scratched on the ground. Folk wisdom says that those who play Sega become poor because they waste so much time.

This girl, living in a cement house near the cemeteries at el-ʿAlamein, has departed from ▷ the Bedouin tradition in adopting a conventional Muslim-style headdress. She has attended only one year of school, while her brothers were sent to school for six years.

A *tisht*, or aluminum washbasin, is part of the modern bride's dowry and has become a necessity in Egyptian villages. In Dakhla Oasis, clothes are washed outdoors, usually in the street. Laundry dries almost immediately in the desert.

In the presence of non-Bedouins, who are presumed not to matter, a Bedouin woman is permitted to remain unveiled. Her downcast eyes represent self-deprecation, deference and modesty Bedouin women from the Western Desert will go to Alexandria unveiled, but among men of their tribe, even relatives, they will cover the lower part of their faces. Older women who have achieved a more elevated and independent status, almost equal to that of men, sometimes choose not to veil.

◁ In the teaching of Islam, there are no priestly intermediaries. Man's relationship with God is direct and private. In Dakhla Oasis, this Muslim offers his sunset prayers to Allah, kneeling on the rooftop of his house. Prayer is the Second Pillar of Islam. Muslims pray in the morning between the moment of dawning until the actual rising of the sun, at high noon, in the late afternoon, at sunset (this prayer may be performed at any time starting four minutes after the sun sinks below the horizon until the last red glow in the sky) and at night. The night prayer is preferably accomplished before midnight. Some prayers are silent, some prayers are recited out loud, and some are mixed. Five times daily, prayer is obligatory, starting at the age of reason, which is considered to be seven years.

Overleaf: Driven by prevailing winds, the sand dunes in the Western Desert inexorably move to the ▷▷ southeast, with the horns of their crescent shapes pointing forward. In five years, the traveling dunes cover as much as two miles. Only the windward side of a dune provides firm footing for camels.

This resident of Farafra Oasis lives in a large, airy house with a sunny courtyard. He weaves rugs made from the wool of his own flock of long-haired sheep. Each rug measures three by five feet and takes a week to weave. Instead of dyeing the rugs, the weavers retain the natural browns and creams of the native sheep. The rugs (not to be confused with the patterned, store-bought floor coverings on the right) feel as soft and silky as cashmere. The weaver earns $24 U.S. a rug for his time spent carding, spinning and weaving. In Farafra, he may have a long, dry spell between customers but he seems happy and prosperous.

This woman lives in Bawiti, capital of Bahriyah Oasis. She was tattooed at age seven. A decorative ▷ tree design runs from her lower lip to her chin. The ocular tattoo on her forehead is designed to ward off the Evil Eye. Tattooers attend village markets and town festivals offering clients a wide choice of designs.

Facade of a house in the village of el-Qasr in Farafra Oasis. The walls are of mud brick which has been plastered over and painted with scenes of desert wildlife and of the pilgrimage to the holy city of Mecca.

This woman is a member of the Awlad 'Ali tribe, the largest ▷ Bedouin group in Egypt's Libyan Desert. She is considered to be a perfect specimen of womanhood—robust, and not too thin.

NOTES

Cairo

1 Ira M. Lapidus. *A History of Islamic Societies.* Cambridge: Cambridge University Press, 1988, p. 347.

2 Stanley Lane-Poole. *The Story of Cairo.* London: J. M. Dent & Co., 1902, pp. 139–140.

3 Bernard Lewis. *The Arabs in History.* New York: Harper & Row, 1958, p. 114.

4 See George Proctor. *History of the Crusades.* Lindsay and Blackstone, 1854, p. 476.

5 For this account, see Elkan N. Adler. *Jewish Travellers.* London: George Routledge and Sons Ltd., 1930.

6 See Roger B. Merriman. *Suleiman the Magnificent.* Cambridge: Cambridge University Press, 1944, p. 130; Philip K. Hitti. *The History of the Arabs.* New York: Macmillan, 1937, (Tenth Edition, 1970), p. 714.

7 André Raymond. *The Great Arab Cities in the 16th to 18th Centuries.* New York: New York University Press, 1984.

8 Alfred J. Butler. *Court Life in Egypt.* London: Chapman and Hall, 1887.

9 John Waterbury. *Egypt: Burdens of the Past, Options For the Future.* Bloomington: Indiana University Press, 1978.

10 A delightful account of the street vendors of Cairo is "The Street Vendors of Cairo" appearing in *Nile Reflections* by Doreen Anwar. Cairo: The American University in Cairo Press, 1986, p. 92.

11 A splendid account of the modernist-traditionalist subway debate appears in Alan Cowell's "Cairo Journal." *New York Times,* January 15, 1990, p. A4.

12 *Qur'an,* translated by Rashad Khalaifa.

13 Valerie J. Hoffman-Ladd of the University of Illinois has published an excellent paper on the controversy over the status of women in contemporary Egypt. Valerie J. Hoffman-Ladd, "Polemics on the Modesty and Segregation of Women in Contemporary Egypt." *International Journal of Middle Eastern Studies,* (1987) p. 23. See particularly her quotation from a representative of the conservative Muslim Brotherhood: "Whoever wishes to know the reason for the progress or backwardness of a nation, let him look at the influence of women on the morals of the sons of the nation . . . for woman is the standard by which the nation rises or falls, and the measure of its greatness or lowliness, and the scale of its courage or cowardice. In truth, one upright mother is better than a thousand teachers."

14 Much of the material on the mores of women in Cairo is drawn from several excellent studies. They are: Diane Singerman, "Avenues of Participation: Family, Politics and Networks in Urban Quarters of Cairo," *Princeton University,* Dissertation, October 1989. See further Alan Cowell, "In Egypt the In-Laws Still Propose," *New York Times,* December 29, 1988.

A good discussion of the classes of women in Cairo is found in Sawson el-Messiri, "Self-Images of Traditional Urban Women in Cairo," appearing in Lois Beck and Nikki Keddie's *Women in the Muslim World,* Cambridge: Harvard University Press, 1978, p. 522; also see "Therapeutic Narratives in Cairo" by Evelyn A. Early, *Social Science Medicine,* 1982, pp. 1491–1492.

15 See Alan Cowell, "Islam in Vogue, Boutiques for the Pious," *New York Times,* July 7, 1990, p. 2A; "Undercover," *Cairo Today,* February 1990, p. 68.

16 For a fine account of men in Cairo, see Unni Wikan, *Life Among the Poor in Cairo,* translated by Ann Henning, London: Tavistock Publications, 1976.

17 For a complete account of the mulid under Sufi Islam, see Ira M. Lapidus. *A History of Islamic Societies.* Cambridge: Cambridge University Press, 1988, p. 195.

Sinai

1 Bernard Lewis. *The Arabs in History.* New York: Harper and Row, 1958, p. 12.

2 William Foxwell Albright. *Archeology and the Religion of Israel.* Baltimore: Johns Hopkins Press, 1968.

3 Joseph J. Hobbs. *Bedouin Life in the Egyptian Wilderness.* Austin: University of Texas Press, 1989, p. 23.

4 T. E. Lawrence. *The Seven Pillars of Wisdom.* London: Jonathan Cape, 1935, p. 41.

5 Larry W. Roeder, Jr. "Tribal Law and Tribal Solidarity in Sinai Bedouin Culture: The Story of Besha," *84 Anthropos,* Fribourg: 1989, p. 230.

6 Burton Bernstein. *Sinai: The Great and Terrible Wilderness.* Austin: University of Texas Press, 1989, p. 102.

7 Joseph J. Hobbs. *Bedouin Life in the Egyptian Wilderness.* Austin: University of Texas Press, 1989, p. 58.

8 Edward H. Palmer. *The Desert of the Exodus.* Cambridge: Deighton, Bell, 1871, p. 96.

9 Edward H. Palmer. *The Desert of the Exodus.* Cambridge: Deighton Bell, 1871, pp. 96–97.

10 Edward H. Palmer. *The Desert of the Exodus.* Cambridge: Deighton, Bell, 1871, pp. 97–98.

11 Edward H. Palmer. *The Desert of the Exodus.* Cambridge: Deighton, Bell, 1871, p. 98.

12 T. E. Lawrence. *The Seven Pillars of Wisdom.* London: Jonathan Cape, 1935, pp. 40–41.

13 For a superb account of the Sinai Bedouin legal system, see *Customary Law in North Sinai,* compiled by the Committee for the Preservation of North Sinai Cultural Heritage, The American University in Cairo Press, 1989.

14 Larry W. Roeder, Jr. "Tribal Law and Tribal Solidarity in Sinai Bedouin Culture: The Story of Besha," *84 Anthropos,* Fribourg: 1989.

15 Burton Bernstein. *Sinai: the Great and Terrible Wilderness.* New York: Viking, 1979, p. 70.

16 Lila Abu-Lughod. "Bedouins, Cassettes and Technologies of Public Culture." Washington: *Middle East Report,* Issue No. 159, (July/August), 1989, p. 10.

17 Burton Bernstein. *Sinai: the Great and Terrible Wilderness.* New York: Viking, 1979, p. 59.

18 Lila Abu-Lughod. *Veiled Sentiments: Honor and Poetry in a Bedouin Society.* Berkeley: University of California Press, 1986, p. 27, pp. 177–185, p. 221.

The Nile Valley

1 Doreen Anwar. *Nile Reflections.* Cairo: The American University in Cairo Press, 1986, p. 16.

2 Herodotus, *Book ii,* p. 34.

3 Louis Werner. "North to Cairo Along the Scorching Way of the Forty." *Smithsonian Magazine,* March 1987, p. 220.

4 *The Iliad.* Translated by Robert Fagles. New York: Viking, 1990, book 9, page 264, line 466.

5 Henry Habib Ayrout. *Fellahs d'Egypte,* Editions du Sphynx, (6th Edition), Le Caire, 1952, p. 16.

6 Henry Habib Ayrout. *Fellahs d'Egypte,* Editions du Sphynx, (6th Edition), Le Caire, 1952, p. 16.

7 Lord Cromer, the British Consul General of Egypt between 1883–1907, declared of the fellah:

Ignorant though he may be, [the fellah] is wise enough to know that he is now far better off than he was prior to the British occupation. He is incapable of establishing clearly in his mind that, for the time being at all events, good administration and the exercise of a paramount influence by England are inseparably linked together.

Cromer, *Modern Egypt.* New York: Macmillan, 1908, Vol. 2, p. 194.

8 Timothy Mitchell. "The Invention and Reinvention of the Egyptian Peasant." New York: *International Journal of Middle Eastern Studies,* 1990.

9 Richard H. Adams, Jr. *Development and Social Change in Rural Egypt.* Syracuse: Syracuse University Press, 1986, p. 83.

10 Naguib Mahfouz. *Midaq Alley,* translated by Trevor Le Gassick. Washington, D.C.: Three Continents Press, 1981, p. 19.

11 Nayra Atiya. *Khul-Khaal: Five Egyptian Women Tell Their Stories.* Cairo: The American University in Cairo Press, 1988, p. 154.

12 Nayra Atiya. *Khul-Khaal: Five Egyptian Women*

Tell Their Stories. Cairo: The American University in Cairo Press, 1988, p. 111.

13 Diane Singerman. "Avenues of Participation: Family, Politics and Networks in Urban Quarters of Cairo." *Princeton University:* Dissertation, October 1989.

14 Andrea B. Rugh, in the foreward to *Khul-Khaal: Five Egyptian Women Tell Their Stories,* by Nayra Atiya, p. xiv.

15 For further information on clitoridectomy practices in Egypt, see Mervat Hatem. "Toward the Study of the Psychodynamics of Mothering and Gender in Egyptian Families." New York: *International Journal of Middle Eastern Studies,* 1987, pp. 287, 298, 300. For additional information on clitoridectomy see an excellent article by Janice Boddy, "The Womb as Oasis: The Symbolic Context of Pharaonic Circumcision in Rural Northern Sudan." *The American Ethnologist,* February 1982, pp. 682–698.

The Boddy paper states: "Here it emerges that female circumcision is intricately related to a wide variety of local customs and beliefs, all of which appear to be informed by several related idioms stressing the relative value of 'enclosedness.' The paper suggests that for those who have undergone it and who advocate its continuance, Pharaonic circumcision is an assertive, highly meaningful act that emphasizes feminine fertility by de-emphasizing female sexuality. [genital mutilation, circumcision, symbolism, women, Sudan, gender]. Pharaonic circumcision, a custom which because of its apparent brutality cannot but horrify the Western intelligence, is for the women of Hofriyat, an assertive symbolic act. Through it they emphasize what they hold to be the essence of femininity: morally appropriate fertility, the potential to reproduce the lineage or to found a lineage section. In that infibulation purifies, smooths, and makes clean the outer surface of the womb, the enclosure or hosh of the house of childbirth, it socializes or, if the phrase be permitted, culturalizes a woman's fertility. Through occlusion of the vaginal orifice, her womb, both literally and figuratively, becomes a social space: enclosed, impervious, virtually impenetrable. Her social virginity, defined by qualities of enclosedness, purity, and all the rest, must periodically be reestablished at those points in her life (after childbirth and before remarriage) when her fertility once again is rendered potent."

16 The marriage contract includes naming the amount of the bride's price, or *mahr,* the bride's engagement presents, *shabka* (usually gold jewelry), and the bride's dowry or *gafsh.* For the signing of the agreement, a registrar, or *maazoon* (a learned man who keeps the official register of marriage and divorce), is called in. The father of the prospective bride enunciates in the reading of the *fatiha:* "I have married my daughter X to Y accepting the payment which the people of the two sides concerned have agreed in the manner prescribed by the Holy Book and the way of the Prophet." See Hamed Ammar, *Growing Up in an Egyptian Village.* London: Routledge and Kegan Paul Ltd., 1954, pp. 193–194.

17 Nayra Atiya. *Khul-Khaal: Five Egyptian Women Tell Their Stories.* Cairo: The American University in Cairo Press, 1988, p. 114.

18 Jehan Sadat. *A Woman of Egypt.* New York: Pocket Books, 1987, p. 50.

19 S. D. Goitein. *A Mediterranean Society.* (2 Volumes). Berkeley: University of California Press, 1967, p. 55.

20 Edward William Lane. *An Account of the Manners and Customs of the Modern Egyptians.* London: J. M. Dent & Sons Ltd., 1836 (reprinted 1966), pp. 504–505.

21 Anthony Sattin. *Letters from Egypt from Florence Nightingale, A Journey on the Nile (1849–1850).* New York: Weidenfeld & Nicolson, 1987, p. 128.

Journey to the Five Oases

1 T.I. Dun. *From Cairo to Siwa:—Across the Libyan Desert with Armoured Cars.* Glasgow: John Smith & Son, 1933, p. 77.

2 Amhed Fakhry. *The Oases of Egypt, Volume I, Siwa Oasis,* quoting Herodotus Book III, p. 26. Cairo: American University in Cairo Press, 1973, p. 26.

3 Ahmed Fakhry. *The Oases of Egypt, Volume I, Siwa Oasis,* Cairo: American University in Cairo Press, 1973, p. 66.

4 In a first-hand account, Oric Bates, describes the procession:
"The god was borne in procession through the palm groves surrounding his Temple. Eighty priests bore on their shoulders a barque (this conveyance betrays at once the Egyptian influence of Amon-Re) on which rested the golden shrine of the Divinity. The barque was ornamented with numerous silver paterae hanging down from the gunwhales (perhaps representing the grave-gear of the dead god) and the image of the god itself was studded with precious stones. A long train of virgins and matrons followed the barque 'singing uncouth hymns in the Libyan tongue, with a view to propitiating the god and inducing him to return to the consultant a satisfactory answer. The diety was carried in the direction in which he himself willed his bearers to go.''
The Eastern Libyans: An Essay, London: Macmillan & Co. Ltd., 1914.

5 Ahmed Fakhry. *The Oases of Egypt, Volume I, Siwa Oasis,* Cairo: American University in Cairo Press, 1973, p. 47.

6 Ahmed Fakhry. *The Oases of Egypt, Volume I, Siwa Oasis,* Cairo: American University in Cairo Press, 1973, p. 43.

7 Ahmed Fakhry. *The Oases of Egypt, Volume I, Siwa Oasis,* Cairo: American University in Cairo Press, 1973, p. 52.

8 Ahmed Fakhry. *The Oases of Egypt, Volume I, Siwa Oasis,* Cairo: American University in Cairo Press, 1973, pp. 62–63.

9 Conversations with Egyptologist Dr. Anthony Mills at Dakhla Oasis, January, 1989.

10 Ahmed Fakhry. *The Oases of Egypt, Volume II, Bahriyah and Farafra Oases,* Cairo: American University in Cairo Press, 1974, p. 46.

11 Ahmed Fakhry. *The Oases of Egypt, Volume II, Bahriyah and Farafra Oases,* Cairo: American University in Cairo Press, 1974, pp. 50–51.

SOURCES AND BIBLIOGRAPHY

Background books and literature on the Western Desert, Sinai, Cairo and Upper Egypt are voluminous and rich. I wish to recognize particularly the following scholars and journalists and express my deep admiration and appreciation for their work. I benefited greatly from the extraordinarily informative and graceful writing of Burton Bernstein. No one in modern times has written more successfully on the "great and terrible wilderness" of the Sinai Peninsula. I am greatly indebted to the scholarship of the renowned Egyptologist, Ahmed Fakhry, the premier authority on the art, archaeology, and the people of the oases of the Western Desert. Throughout my research, I gained perspective and wisdom from the eminent Islamic historian, Professor Bernard Lewis. I am indebted to anthropologist Lila Abu-Lughod, whose widely-acclaimed writings have revealed a deep and sensitive understanding of the culture and psyche of Bedouin women.

Both desert sections of this book benefited from the work of the distinguished ethnographer, Professor Joseph Hobbs. In my research, I often turned to Winifred Blackman and her wonderfully descriptive material on folk customs and superstitions. An always invaluable source was the classic text by the great Edward W. Lane who so comprehensively chronicled life and customs in nineteenth-century Egypt. For additional information on Siwa Oasis, I often turned to the charming and chatty writings of Major T. I. Dun and the vivid and moving accounts of C. Dalrymple Belgrave. I benefited from the work of Valerie J. Hoffman-Ladd who so skillfully explained and documented the return by many Egyptian women to Islamic dress and traditions. At times, I relied on the work of distinguished anthropologist, Donald Powell Cole, for Bedouin tribal life. I looked to the work of Sawsan-el Messiri for insights on the self-images of traditional women in Cairo and their perceptions of the ideal husband.

In my account of life along the Nile, I was greatly helped by Denis Boyles's delightful account of the River below the Sudan and in Upper Egypt. I was aided by Janice Boddy for her esteemed and objective account of female circumcision practices in Upper Egypt and the Sudan. I turned to the superb work of anthropologist Andrea B. Rugh as a source, particularly her widely respected insights into the roles of women and family solidarity. I often made use of Shirley Kay's distinguished ethnological work on Bedouin life in "the black tent." For the history of Cairo in the medieval period, I referred to the important work of the distinguished urban sociologist, Janet Abu-Lughod. At many points I am indebted to Alan Cowell whose superb reporting on such diverse subjects as Islamic dress, Ramadan, Cairo's City of the Dead, camels, child laborers, and the Cairo subway are always deeply revealing. I am indebted to the research and wisdom of Wedad Zénié-Ziegler who has so movingly described the profound loneliness and serenity of peasant women both in Nile villages and in the poorer districts of Cairo. I often turned to the reporting of Tony Walker of the *Financial Times* who has written with great insight on many issues in Egypt, particularly on veiling and "Islamic chic."

My section on life in the Nile Valley drew on the work of Peter J. Awn for current devotional practices in Ramadan and on the *Hajj.* An always dependable source was John Kifner of the *New York Times* who has consistently produced distinguished and subtle reporting from Cairo. I was helped by Professor Timothy Mitchell's clear visions of social and economic change among the *fellahin* of the Nile Valley. I drew on the work of Alan Moorehead and Geoffrey Moorehouse for their splendid writings on the geography and culture of the upper Nile. I often turned to the late Robin Fedden for his superbly readable accounts of medieval Cairo and of contemporary life in the villages and the oases of the Western Desert. I am indebted to Doreen Anwar of the American University in Cairo for her sensitive impressions of such topics as street vendors and mothers-in-law.

I am indebted to Egyptian writer and painter, Nayra Atiya, for recording oral histories about failed marriages, unrequited love, the death of a child, and other calamities afflicting lower-class women in Cairo. For Sinai and the Western Desert, I often turned to George William Murray for his brilliant and comprehensive studies of the customs and beliefs of Bedouin tribes. An important source of Bedouin lore and superstition, particularly in South Sinai, was nineteenth-century British Arabist, Edward H. Palmer. On the habits and culture of the Egyptian peasant in the Nile villages, I have used the work of two outstanding scholars of the subject, Hamed Ammar and Henry Ayrout. I am indebted to the political economist, Richard Adams, for reports of contemporary conditions in agricultural Egypt. For my story on the path of the Nile, I benefited from that poet of history and Nile River life, Emil Ludwig.

Few sources have been as valuable to me as Professor Diane Singerman, author of a brilliant dissertation on the role of family celebrations, traditions and rituals as they solidify and empower the lives of people in the poor sections of Cairo. My account of medieval Cairo under the Fatimids, Mamluks and 'Ayyubids follows the classic work by Stanley Lane-Poole who wrote at the turn of the century. For definitive information on Islamic monuments in Cairo, I have relied on the universally praised and standard work of Richard B. Parker, Robin Sabin, and Caroline Williams. Last, I wish to mention Philip K. Hitti, whose incomparable text on Arab-speaking peoples (now in its tenth edition) has been my constant guide.

References to other works I used and consulted will be found in the bibliography that follows. These include texts, newspaper articles and academic journals.

Bibliography

Abu-Lughod, Janet. *Cairo: 1001 Years of the City Victorious*. Princeton: Princeton University Press, 1971.

Abu-Lughod, Lila. *Veiled Sentiments: Honor and Poetry in a Bedouin Society*. Berkeley: University of California Press, 1986.

Abu-Lughod, Lila. "Aestheticized Emotions & Critical Hermeneutics." Dordrecht, Netherlands: *Culture, Medicine and Psychiatry*, 1988.

Abu-Lughod, Lila. "Bedouin Blues." *Natural History*, July, 1987.

Abu-Lughod, Lila. "Bedouins, Cassettes and Technologies of Public Culture." Washington: *Middle East Report*, July/Aug, 1989.

Adams, Richard H., Jr. *Development and Social Change in Rural Egypt*. Syracuse: Syracuse University Press, 1986.

Adler, Elkan N. *Jewish Travellers*. London: George Routledge and Sons, 1930.

Ahmed, Akbar S. *Discovering Islam: Making Sense of Muslim History and Society*. London: Routledge and Kegan Paul, 1988.

Al-Hilw, Kamal Abdallah, and Said Mumtaz Darwish. *Customary Law in Northern Sinai*. Cairo: Printshop of The American University in Cairo, 1989.

Al-Sayyid Marsot, and Afaf Lutfi. "Popular Attitudes Towards Authority in Egypt." Fresno: *Journal of Arab Affairs*, 1988.

Alafenish, Salim. "Processes of Change and Continuity in Kinship System and Family Ideology in Bedouin Society." Assen, Netherlands: *Sociologia Ruralis*, 1987.

Albright, William Foxwell. *Archeology and the Religion of Israel*. Baltimore: Johns Hopkins University Press, 1969.

Aldridge, James. *Cairo*. Boston: Little, Brown and Company, 1969.

Ammar, Hamed. *Growing Up in an Egyptian Village*. London: Routledge and Kegan Paul, 1954.

Anwar, Doreen. *Nile Reflections*. Cairo: The American University in Cairo Press, 1986.

Atiya, Nayra. *Khul-Khaal: Five Egyptian Women Tell Their Stories*. Cairo: The American University in Cairo Press, 1988.

Awn, Peter J. *The Religious and Political Life of a World Community*. New York: Praeger, 1984.

Awn, Peter J. *Islam Faith and Practice*. New York: Praeger, 1984.

Ayrout, Henry Habid. *Fellahs d'Egypte*, 6th edition. Le Caire: Editions du Sphynx, 1952.

Baedeker. *Baedeker's Egypt*. Englewood Cliffs, NJ: Prentice-Hall, Inc., 1988.

Bartlett, W.H. *The Nile Boat: or Glimpses of the Land of Egypt*. London: Arthur Hall, Virtue, And Co., 1850.

Bates, Oric. *The Eastern Libyans: An Essay*. London: Macmillan and Co., 1914.

Beadnell, H.J. Llewellyn. *An Egyptian Oasis: An Account of the Oasis of Kharga in the Libyan Desert*. London: John Murray, 1909.

Beck, Lois and Nikki Keddie. *Women in the Muslim World*. Cambridge, Mass. and London, England: Harvard University Press, 1978.

Belgrave, C. Dalrymple. *Siwa: The Oasis of Jupiter Ammon*. London: John Lane The Bodley Head, 1923.

Bell, Lanny. "Luxor Temple and the Cult of the Royal Ka." *Journal of Near Eastern Studies*. 44, (1985). pp. 251–294.

Bell, Lanny. "The Epigraphic Survey and the Rescue of the Monuments of Ancient Egypt." In *The Ancient Eastern Meditteranean: Centennial Symposium, 1889–1989*, edited by Eleanor Guralnick. Chicago: The Chicago Society of the Archeological Institute of America, 1990, pp. 7–15.

Bernstein, Burton. *Sinai: The Great and Terrible Wilderness*. New York: Viking, 1979.

Bey, A.M. Hassanein. *The Lost Oases*. London: Thornton Butterworth, 1925.

Blackman, Winifred S. *The Fellahin of Upper Egypt*. London: George G. Harrap and Company, 1927.

Boddy, Janice. "Womb as Oasis: The Symbolic Context of Pharaonic Circumcision in Rural Northern Sudan." Washington: *American Ethnologist*, 1982, pp. 682–698.

Bouverie, Jasper Pleydell. "Siwa: Under Siege." *Cairo Today*, February 1989.

Boyles, Denis. *African Lives*. New York: Weidenfield & Nicolson, 1988.

Braudel, Fernand. *The Mediterranean: and the Mediterranean World in the Age of Philip I*, Volume I. Translated by Sian Reynolds. New York: Harper and Row, 1972.

Brockelmann, Carl. *History of the Islamic Peoples*. Translated by Joel Carmichael and Moshe Perlmann. London: Routledge and Kegan Paul, 1948.

Brown, Nathan J. *Peasant Politics in Modern Egypt*. New Haven: Yale University Press, 1990.

Bucht, Birgitta and M.A. El Badry. "Reflections on Recent Levels and Trends of Fertility and Mortality in Egypt," *Population Studies*, 40, 1986, pages 101–113.

Butler, Alfred J. *Court Life in Egypt*. London: Chapman and Hall, 1887.

Cole, Donald Powell. *Nomads of the Nomads: The Al Murrah Bedouin of the Empty Quarter*. Chicago: Aldine Publishing Company, 1975.

Courtright, P., J. Sheppard, J. Schacter, M.E. Said, and C. R. Dawson. "Trachoma and Blindness in the Nile Delta: Current Patterns and Projections for the Future in the Rural Egyptian Population." London: *British Journal of Opthalmology*, 1989.

Cowell, Alan. "Cairo Journal," *New York Times*, January 15, 1990, p. A4.

Cowell, Alan. "In Egypt the In-Laws Still Propose," *New York Times*, December 29, 1988.

Cowell, Alan. "Islam in Vogue, Boutiques for the Pious," *New York Times*, July 7, 1990, p. A2.

Cowell, Alan. "Staying on the Safe Side," *New York Times*, June 7, 1990.

Cowell, Alan. "Exploring Islamic Cairo," *New York Times*, January 1, 1989.

Cowell, Alan. "Undercover," *Cairo Today*, February 1990, p. 68.

Cowell, Alan. "Underground Pollution Imperils Egypt's Relics," *New York Times*, January 7, 1990.

Cullinan, Sue. "What's Doing in Cairo." *New York Times*, March 7, 1990.

Dart, John. "Arabs a Minority in World's Second-Largest Religion," *Los Angeles Times*, January 24, 1991.

Dickson, H.R.P. *The Arab of the Desert*. London: George Allen and Unwin, Revised Edition, 1983.

Dun, Major T.I. *From Cairo to Siwa, Across the Libyan Desert by Armored Car*. London: John Smith and Son, 1933.

Early, Evelyn A. "Catharsis and Creation: The Everyday Narratives of Baladi Women of Cairo," *Anthropology Quarterly*, Washington, 1985.

Early, Evelyn A. "The Logic of Well Being: Therapeutic Narratives in Cairo," *Social Science Medicine*, 1982, pp. 1491–1497.

El-Baz, Farouk. "Egypt's Desert of Promise," *National Geographic* No. 2, Vol. 161, February, 1982.

El-Messiri, Sawsan. "Self-Images of Traditional Urban Women in Cairo" appearing in Lois Beck, and Nikki Keddie's *Women in the Muslim World*. Cambridge: Harvard University Press, 1978.

Fagles, Robert, trans. Homer's *The Iliad*. New York: Viking, 1990. Book 9.

Fakhry, Ahmed. *The Oases of Egypt: Volume I, Siwa Oasis*. Cairo: The American University in Cairo Press, 1973.

Fakhry, Ahmed. *The Oases of Egypt: Volume II, Bahriyah and Farafra Oases*. Cairo: The American University in Cairo Press, 1974.

Fakhry, Ahmed. *The Oasis of Siwa: Its Customs, History and Monuments*. Cairo: Wadi El-Nil Press, 1950.

Fakhry, Ahmed. *Recent Explorations in the Oases of the Western Desert*. Cairo: Press of the French Institute of Oriental Archaeology, 1942.

Fedden, Robin. *Egypt: Land of the Valley*. London: Michael Haag Limited, 1977.

Fernea, Elizabeth Warnock and Basima Qattan Bezirgan. *Middle Eastern Muslim Women Speak*. Austin and London: University of Texas Press, 1977.

Fluehr-Lobban, Carolyn and Lois Bardsley-Sirois. "Obedience (Ta-a) in Muslim Marriage: Religious Interpretation and Applied Law in Egypt." Calgary: *Journal of Comparative Family Studies*, 1990.

Gershoni, Israel and James Jankowski. *Egypt, Islam and the Arabs: The Search for Egyptian Nationhood, 1900–1930*. New York: Oxford University Press, 1989.

Ghosh, Amitav. "Pharaohs, and Phantoms." New York: *New Republic*, June 5, 1989, page 33.

Glassé, Cyril. *The Concise Encyclopedia of Islam*. New York: Harper and Row, 1989.

Goitein, S.D. *Letters of Medieval Jewish Traders*. Princeton: Princeton University Press, 1973.

Goitein, S.D. *A Mediterranean Society*, Volume I. Berkeley and Los Angeles: University of California Press, 1967.

Goldberg, Ellis. *Tinker, Tailor and Textile Worker: Class and Politics in Egypt, 1930–1952*. Berkeley: University of California Press, 1986.

Golding, William. *An Egyptian Journal*. London: Faber and Faber, 1985.

Goodman, Steven M. and Peter L. Meininger, Sherif M. Baha el Din, Joseph J. Hobbs, Wim C. Mullie. *The Birds of Egypt*. Oxford: Oxford University Press, 1989.

Hassan, Fathy. *Gourna: A Tale of Two Villages*. Cairo: Ministry of Culture Publications (1969).

Hatem, Mervat. "Toward the Study of the Psychodynamics of Mothering and Gender in Egyptian Families." New York: *International Journal of Middle Eastern Studies*, 1987.

Henein, Nessim Henry. *Mari Girgis: Village de Haute-Egypte*. Cairo: Institut Francais D'Archeologie Orientale Du Caire, 1988.

Hewison, R. Neil. *The Fayoum: A Practical Guide*. Cairo: The American University in Cairo Press, 1985.

Hitti, Philip K. *History of The Arabs: From the Earliest Times to the Present*. New York: Macmillan, 1970.

Hobbs, Joseph J. *Bedouin Life in the Egyptian Wilderness*. Austin: University of Texas Press, 1989.

Hoefer, Hans Johannes. *Egypt*. Singapore: APA Publications (HK) Ltd., 1988.

Hoffman-Ladd, Valerie J. "Polemics on the Modesty and Segregation of Women in Contemporary Egypt," *International Journal of Middle Eastern Studies*, 1987, p. 23.

Ibrahim, Saad Eddin and Donald P. Cole. *The Cairo Papers in Social Science, Monograph Five: Saudi Arabian Bedouin: An Assessment of Their Needs*. Cairo, American University in Cairo Press, 1978.

Ingham, Bruce. *Bedouin of Northern Arabia: Traditions of the Al-Dhafir*. London: KPI, 1986.

Jarvis, Major C.S. *Three Deserts*. London: John Murray, 1936.

Jarvis, Major C.S. *Yesterday and Today in Sinai*. Boston: Houghton Mifflin Company, 1932.

Kamil, Jill. *Coptic Egypt: History and Guide*. Cairo: The American University in Cairo Press, 1987.

Katakura, Motoko. *Bedouin Village: A Study of a Saudi Arabian People in Transition*. Tokyo: University of Tokyo Press, 1977.

Kay, Shirley. *The Bedouin: This Changing World*. New York: Crane, Russak and Company Inc., 1978.

Kepel, Gilles. *The Prophet and the Pharaoh: Muslim Extremism in Egypt.* London: Al Saqi Books, 1985.

Kelly, Marjorie. *Islam: The Religious and Political Life of a World Community.* New York: Praeger Special Studies, 1984.

Khalaifa, Rashad. (*Qur'an*) translation.

Khaldun, ibn. *The Muqaddimah: An Introduction to History.* Translated from the Arabic by Franz Rosenthal. New York: Pantheon Books, 1958.

King, W.J. Harding. *Mysteries of the Libyan Desert.* London: Seeley Service and Co., 1925.

Lane, Edward William. *An Account of the Manners and Customs of the Modern Egyptians.* The Hague: East-West Publications, 1836 (first published 1836, republished 1989).

Lane-Poole, Stanley. *The Story of Cairo.* London: J.M. Dent & Co., 1902.

Lane-Poole, Stanley. *Egypt.* London: Sampson Low, Marston, Searle and Rivington, 1881.

Lapidus, Ira M. *A History of Islamic Societies.* Cambridge: Cambridge University Press, 1988.

Lavie, Smadar. *The Poetics of Military Occupation; Mzeina Allegories of Bedouin Identity Under Israeli and Egyptian Rule.* Berkeley, Los Angeles, Oxford: University of California Press, 1990.

Lawrence, T.E. *The Seven Pillars of Wisdom.* London: Jonathan Cape, 1935.

Leeder, S.H. *Modern Sons of the Pharaohs.* New York: Arno Press, 1973.

Lenoir, Paul. *The Fayoum: or Artists in Egypt.* London: Henry S. King and Co., 1873.

Lewis, Bernard. *The Arabs in History.* New York: Harper and Row, 1958.

Ludwig, Emil. *The Nile: The Life-Story of a River.* Translated by Mary H. Lindsay. New York: Viking, 1937.

MacLeod, Arlene Elowe. *Accommodating Protest: Working Women, the New Veiling, and Change in Cairo.* New York: Columbia University Press, 1991.

Mahfouz, Naguib. *Midaq Alley.* Translated by Trevor Le Gassic. Washington, D.C.: Three Continents Press, 1981.

Mann, Mimi, "King Tut's Tomb Being Reborn In All Its Glitter," *Los Angeles Times,* December 7, 1990.

Marlowe, John. *Four Aspects of Egypt.* London: George Allen and Unwin, 1966.

Marx, Emanuel. *Bedouin of the Negev.* Manchester: Manchester University Press, 1967.

Meir, Avinoam. "Nomads and the State: the Spatial Dynamics of Centrifugal and Centripetal Forces Among the Israeli Negev Bedouin," *Political Geography Quarterly,* Vol. 7, No. 3, July 1988, pages 251–270.

Mitchell, Timothy. "The Invention and Reinvention of the Egyptian Peasant." New York: *International Journal of Middle Eastern Studies,* 1990.

Moorehead, Alan. *The Blue Nile.* London: Hamish Hamilton, 1962.

Moorehead, Alan. *The White Nile.* New York: Vintage Books, 1987.

Murray, G.W. *Sons of Ishmael: A Study of the Egyptian Bedouin.* London: George Routledge and Sons, 1935.

Nightingale, Florence. *Letters from Egypt: A Journey on the Nile, 1849–1850.* New York: Weidenfeld and Nicolson, 1987.

Nomachi, Kazuyoshi. *The Nile.* Introduction by Geoffrey Moorehouse. Boston: Little, Brown and Company, 1988.

Nomachi, Kazuyoshi. *Sinai.* New York: Everest House, 1975.

Palmer, E.H. *The Desert of the Exodus: Journeys on Foot in the Wilderness of the Forty Years' Wanderings.* Part I, Part II. Cambridge: Deighton, Bell and Co. 1871.

Parker, Richard B. and Robin Sabin. *Islamic Monuments in Cairo: A Practical Guide.* Revised by Caroline Williams. Cairo: The American University in Cairo Press, 1985.

Perevolotsky, Avi. "Territoriality and Resource Sharing Among the Bedouin of Southern Sinai: A Socio-Ecological Interpretation," *Journal of Arid Environments* (1987).

Perevolotsky, Avi, Ayelet Perevolotsky and Immanuel Nov-Meir. "Environmental Adaptation and Economic Change in a Pastoral Mountain Society: the Case of the Jabaliyah Bedouin of the Mt. Sinai Region," *Mountain Research and Development,* Vol. 9, No. 2, 1989, pp. 153–164.

Petry, Carl F. *The Civilian Elite of Cairo in the Later Middle Ages.* Princeton: Princeton University Press, 1981.

Raymond, André. *The Great Arab Cities in the 16th to 18th Centuries.* New York: New York University Press, 1984.

Reynolds-Ball, Eustace A. *The City of the Caliphs: A Popular Study of Cairo and Its Environs and the Nile and Its Antiquities.* Boston: Dana Estes and Company, 1897.

Richards, Alan and Philip L. Martin. *Migration, Mechanization, and Agricultural Labor Markets in Egypt.* Boulder: Westview Press, 1983.

Rodinson, Maxime. *Muhammad.* New York: Pantheon Books, 1971.

Roeder, Larry W., Jr. "Tribal Law and Tribal Solidarity in Sinai Bedouin Culture: The Story of Besha." Fribourg: *Anthropos,* 1989.

Rugh, Andreas B. *Family in Contemporary Egypt.* Cairo: The American University in Cairo Press, 1985.

Rugh, Andrea B. *Reveal and Congeal: Dress in Contemporary Egypt.* Cairo: The American University in Cairo Press, 1987.

Rugh, Andrea B. *Religious Community and Social Control In A Lower-Class Area of Cairo.* Cairo: The American University in Cairo Press, 1978.

Russell, Norman. *The Lives of the Desert Fathers: The Historia Monachorum in Aegypto.* London: A.R. Mowbray and Co., 1980.

Sadat, Jehan. *A Woman of Egypt.* New York: Pocket Books, 1987.

Saleh, Heba. "To Work Or Not To Work," *Cairo Today,* February 1990, pages 68, 69.

Saunders, Lucie Wood and Soheir Mehenna. "Village Entrepreneurs: An Egyptian Case." Pittsburgh: *Ethnology,* 1986.

Shaarawi, Huda. *Harem Years: The Memoirs of an Egyptian Feminist (1879–1924).* London: Virago Press, 1986.

Shipler, David K. *Arab and Jew: Wounded Spirits in a Promised Land.* New York: Penguin Books, 1986.

Shorter, Frederic. "Cairo's Leap Forward: People, Households, and Dwelling Space." *Cairo Papers in Social Science,* Volume 12, Monograph 1, Spring 1989.

Simpson, G.E. *The Heart of Libya: The Siwa Oasis, Its People, Customs and Sport.* London: H.F. and G. Witherby, 1929.

Singerman, Diane. "Avenues of Participation: Family, Politics and Networks in Urban Quarters of Cairo." Princeton University: Dissertation, October 1989.

Smith, Jack. "Heat, Dust and 'Bucksheesh' Didn't Stop In Luxor." *Los Angeles Times,* May 29, 1990.

Smith, Jack. "In Cairo, Even the Dead Have to Share Living Space." *Los Angeles Times,* May 7, 1990.

Soliman, Ahmed. "Housing the Urban Poor in Egypt: a Critique of Present Policies," *International Journal of Urban and Regional Research,* 1988, pages 65–86.

Soueif, M.I., Z.A. Darweesh, M.A. Hannourah, A.M. El-Sayfd, F.A. Yunis, and H.S. Taha. "The Extent of Drug Use Among Egyptian Male University Students." Ireland: *Drug and Alcohol Dependence,* 1986.

Stark, Freya. *The Journey's Echo.* New York: Ecco Press, 1988.

Thurston, Harry. "Everlasting Oasis," *Equinox,* Sept./Oct., 1987.

Toubia, Nahid. *Women of the Arab World: The Coming Challenge.* Translated by Nahed El Gamal. London: Zed Books, 1988.

Tuma, Elias H. "Institutionalized Obstacles to Development: The Case of Egypt." Oxford: *World Development,* 1988.

Van Ess, Dorothy. *Fatima and Her Sisters.* New York: John Day Company, 1961.

Vatikiotis, P.J. *The History of Egypt.* Baltimore: Johns Hopkins University Press, 1980.

Vielle, Paul. "Family Alliances and Sexual Politics," Women in the Muslim World, edited by Lois Beck and Nikki Keddie. Cambridge: *Harvard University Press,* 1978, pp. 459 et seq.

Von Dumreicher, Andre. *Trackers & Smugglers in The Deserts of Egypt.* London: Methuen and Co., 1931.

Walker, Tony. "Egypt Yields More Treasure." London: *Financial Times,* April 20, 1989.

Walker, Tony. "New Riddle for Conservationists." London: *Financial Times,* May 19, 1990.

Waterbury, John. *The Egypt of Nasser and Sadat: The Political Economy of Two Regimes.* Princeton: Princeton University Press, 1983.

Waterbury, John. *Egypt: Burdens of the Past, Options for the Future.* Bloomington: Indiana University Press, 1978.

Waterbury, John. *Egypt: Burdens of the Past/Visions for the Future.* Bloomington: American University Field Staff, Indiana University, 1978.

Weideger, Paula. "Coping with Egypt on Your Own." *New York Times,* January 1, 1989.

Wenke, Robert J. "Egypt: Origins of Complex Societies." Palo Alto: *Annual Reviews Anthropology,* 1989.

Werner, Louis. "North to Cairo along the Scorching Way of the Forty." *Smithsonian Magazine,* March 1987, p. 220.

White, Arthur Silva. *From Sphinx to Oracle: Through the Libyan Desert to the Oasis of Jupiter Ammon.* London: Hurst and Blackett, 1899.

Wiet, Gaston. *Cairo: City of Art and Commerce.* Translated by Seymour Feiler. Norman, Okla.: University of Oklahoma Press, 1964.

Wikan, Unni. *Life Among the Poor in Cairo.* Translated by Anne Henning. London: Tavistock Publications, 1976.

Wikan, Unni. "Bereavement and Loss in Two Muslim Communities: Egypt and Bali Compared," *Social Science Medicine,* Vol. 27, No. 5, pp. 451–460, 1988.

Wikan, Unni. *Behind the Veil in Arabia.* Baltimore: Johns Hopkins University Press, 1982.

Wikan, Unni. "Living Conditions among Cairo's Poor—A View from Below." *Middle East Journal,* 1985 39(1):7–26.

Wilkinson, Sir Gardner, F.R.S. *Hand-Book for Travellers in Egypt.* London: John Murray, 1847.

Williams, Caroline. "Islamic Cairo; Endangered Legacy," *The Middle East Journal,* Volume 39, No. 3, Summer 1985, pages 231–246.

Zénié-Ziegler, Wedad. *In Search of Shadows: Conversations with Egyptian Women.* London: Zed Books, 1988.

JUNE TOWER

About the Author

Mary Cross is a photojournalist and portrait photographer. Educated at Hollins College, Sweet Briar College and the Sorbonne, she studied portrait photography with Philippe Halsman.

Her photographs of the Bedouin tribes of Sinai and the Oases of the Western Desert of Egypt were exhibited in the Fall of 1990 at Princeton University under the auspices of the Woodrow Wilson School and the University's Program in Near Eastern Studies. Later exhibitions of her work in Egypt are to appear at Harvard University and at the National Humanities Center.

Her photographs of China, taken shortly after that country opened to the West, appeared in her book, *Behind the Great Wall—A Photographic Essay on China* (Atheneum 1979). Her portraits of China were exhibited at the Los Angeles County Museum of Natural History and the J.B. Speed Art Museum, Louisville, Kentucky.

The author was born in Louisville, Kentucky in 1936. She lives in Princeton, New Jersey with her husband, Theodore Cross, a publisher. She is the mother of three grown daughters.

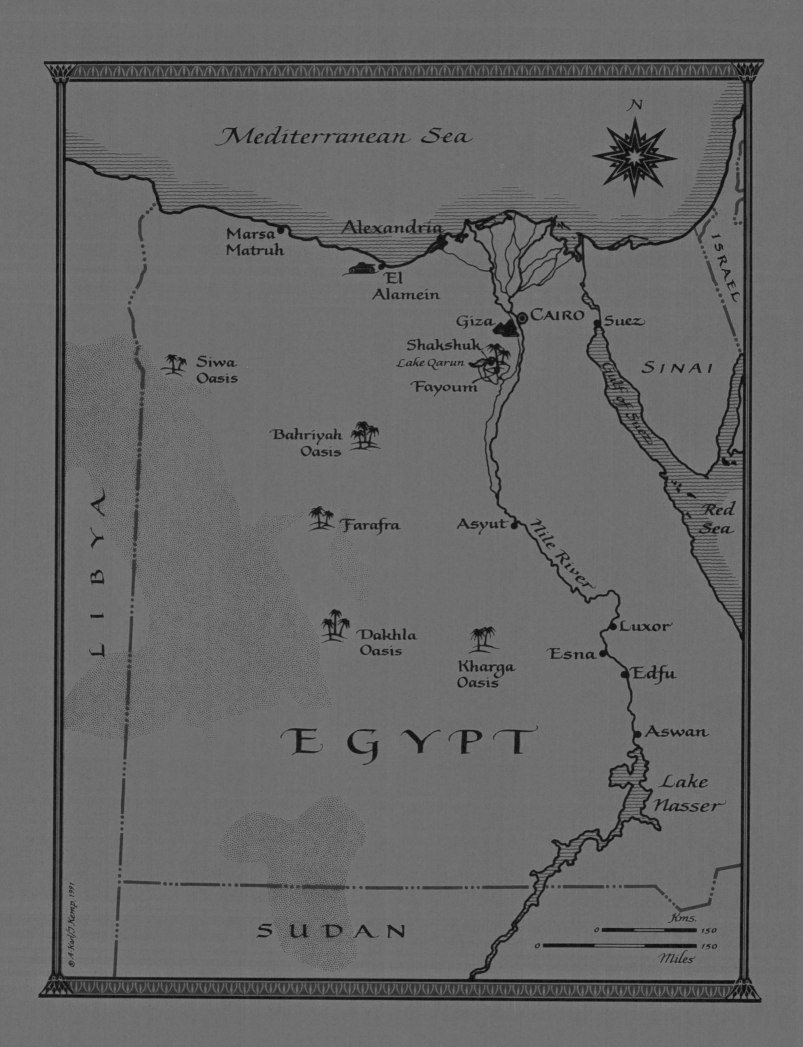